MOUNTAIN STATES
POLICY MANUAL

2024 Edition

Dear friends,

Policies have consequences. Ideas have lasting impact.

The *Mountain States Policy Manual* – published by the staff of Mountain States Policy Center – is an in-depth guide intended to serve as a resource for citizens, policymakers, the media and those who wish to improve the lives of citizens in Idaho, Montana, Wyoming and Washington state.

We present these recommendations based on years of research and insight. Now more than ever, free-market successes need to be communicated effectively in the marketplace of ideas.

Mountain States Policy Center is an independent, free market think tank based. We are not beholden to any government bureaucrat or special interest group. We produce ideas based on facts, not emotion.

This policy manual will offer citizens many practical ideas and hope for the future. It will provide media with background and research needed to improve accuracy. And it will offer policymakers of any political persuasion a go-to resource for navigating key issues facing the Mountain West, all rooted in proven, free market solutions.

We invite you to join Mountain States Policy Center with a tax-deductible contribution. Thank you for your support of our work and for putting Free Markets First.

Chris Cargill
Founder, President & CEO

PRINCIPLES

Mountain States Policy Center (MSPC) was founded in 2022 to empower individuals to succeed through non-partisan, quality research that promotes free enterprise, individual liberty and limited government.

With a headquarters in Idaho and coverage in Washington state, Montana, and Wyoming, MSPC is the first multi-state think tank of its kind, working to educate key segments of society — including policymakers, the media, young leaders, and the rising generation of citizens — on the power of free markets and limited government to unleash prosperity and opportunity throughout the Mountain West and the nation. We believe in a core set of principles:

- ☐ Government should be limited and focused on core functions

- ☐ Where there is competition and freedom of choice, outcomes improve

- ☐ Private property rights are essential to a free society

- ☐ The price of goods and services should be determined by supply and demand

- ☐ Policymakers should focus on incentives rather than coercion

- ☐ Regulations should be practical, predictable and limited

- ☐ Freedom of speech and the marketplace of ideas should never be curtailed

Readers of our work will see certain economic and governance terms used frequently. To help provide context for our analysis and recommendations, here is a description of what these terms mean.

Capitalism – *An economic system driven by individual actors using market factors (supply and demand) to determine the free exchange of goods and services, rather than economic activity dictated by central government control and intervention. A hallmark of capitalism is private ownership of both property and the means of production.*

Communism – *An economic system developed by Karl Marx that focuses on class warfare with the goal of government ownership of all property and centralized planning of economic activity. The theory of communism is that each person will work and be paid based on their abilities and needs instead of the economic value of their actual production.*

Core functions of government – *The core functions of government are those activities not easily replicated in the private sector such as public safety, coordinated infrastructure, general order, and the protection of private property and individual rights.*

Education choice – *Education choice is the principle that parents, no matter their economic status, should have the ability to choose how best to educate their children. Education choice options include the freedom to attend any public school (not be limited by zip code), public charter schools, private schools, homeschooling, Education Savings Accounts, and other tools that empower parents to meet the individual educational needs of their child. Education choice recognizes that families and parents are in the best position to determine the individual educational needs for their child's success.*

Federalism – *Federalism is the governing process that defines specific limited powers for the federal government with the remaining governing authority reserved for state governments. The U.S. Constitution embraces a balance of power shared by the national and state governments. The strong role provided for local governance is protected by the 10th Amendment.*

Free market/enterprise – *The free market/enterprise is best understood as an economic system that allows individual actors to voluntarily engage in the exchange of goods and services with prices determined by supply and demand instead of government restrictions. A key component of a free market is voluntary economic activity instead of government coercion on the exchange of goods or services.*

DEFINITIONS

Individual liberty – *The concept of individual liberty is the freedom to make decisions for oneself and exercise control over daily activities free from undue government control or manipulation. The role of the government in a system that respects individual liberty is to limit any intrusions only to those activities that protect individuals from the encroachment of actions from others.*

Limited government – *Under a system of limited government, legal restrictions are placed on government bodies and officials to avoid abuses of power and consolidation of influence.*

Open government – *The foundations for an accountable government can be found in strong citizen oversight, and one of the most critical tools for this goal is open government laws. Requirements for access to public records, open meetings, public comment periods, and legislative transparency are critical tools necessary for citizens to maintain control over the government they have created.*

Republican form of government – *Power held by the people and not a select few is the underpinning of a republican form of government. Citizens elect representatives to serve the public interest and the government remains responsive to the people via regular elections to reflect the will of the electorate.*

Separation of powers – *A critical protection to avoid government abuse is the separation of powers. This is commonly referred to as checks and balances and is a division of government power and responsibility between distinct branches of government to prevent the concentration of power in the hands of a few.*

Socialism – *Socialism is a political and economic system that provides the government with the authority to make all economic decisions about the production and distribution of goods and services. Under socialism, some private control and ownership of resources are allowed, whereas under communism everything is owned by the government.*

TABLE OF CONTENTS

TABLE OF CONTENTS

Chapter 4: Education

Chapter 5: Economic & Business Climate

Chapter 6: Health care

Chapter 7: Technology & Innovation

TABLE OF CONTENTS

I. Require a supermajority vote for state and local tax increases

If there's one thing Americans can still agree on it's that tax policy is one of the most consequential decisions our government makes, impacting the economy and family budgets. There is also general agreement that tax increases should be a last resort when budgeting and imposing them should not be taken lightly by policymakers.

One way to ensure this occurs is by adding requirements to a state's constitution that require a supermajority vote or voter approval to raise taxes. This type of taxpayer protection already exists in several states.

Supermajority vote requirements by state
As of 2024

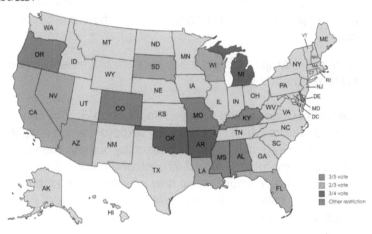

Examples

There are currently 17 states with some form of supermajority or voter approval requirements for tax increases.[1] Here are examples of the legislative vote thresholds required to raise taxes in those states:

- ☐ 3/5 vote: Delaware, Kentucky, Mississippi, and Oregon.

- ☐ 2/3 vote: Arizona, California (includes fee increases), Florida, Louisiana, Nevada (includes fee increases), South Dakota, and Wisconsin.

- ☐ 3/4 vote: Arkansas, Michigan (property taxes only), and Oklahoma.

- ☐ Other: Alabama (state income and property taxes cannot be increased without a constitutional amendment), Colorado (voter approval is required for all tax increases), and Missouri (voter approval is required to raise taxes above a set revenue cap).

Here are examples of how these tax restrictions are worded in state constitutions:

- ☐ **California Constitution Article 13a, Section 3:** "Any change in state statute which results in any taxpayer paying a higher tax must be imposed by an act passed by not less than two-thirds of all members elected to each of the two houses of the Legislature, except that no new ad valorem taxes on real property, or sales or transaction taxes on the sales of real property may be imposed."[2]

---

[1] "Senate considers supermajority for taxes constitutional amendments," Washington Policy Center, February 2013, available at https://www.washingtonpolicy.org/publications/detail/senate-considers-supermajority-for-taxes-constitutional-amendments

[2] "California Constitution Article XIII A - Tax Limitation Section 3," Justia Law, accessed on October 23, 2023, available at https://law.justia.com/constitution/california/article-xiii-a/section-3/

☐ **South Dakota Constitution Article 11, Section 14**: "Vote required to impose or increase taxes. The rate of taxation imposed by the State of South Dakota in regard to any tax may not be increased and no new tax may be imposed by the State of South Dakota unless by consent of the people by exercise of their right of initiative or by two-thirds vote of all the members elect of each branch of the Legislature."[3]

Proactively acting to protect taxpayers by sending voters a supermajority for tax increases constitutional amendment is a prudent thing for policymakers to do. Whether requiring voter approval for all tax increases like in Colorado or needing a 2/3 legislative threshold as occurs in Florida, increasing the tax burden imposed on families and businesses should first secure a broad consensus and always be the last resort when budgeting.

VIDEO: We need supermajority tax protection

II. **Use performance-based budgeting to focus taxpayer dollars on expected outcomes**

When taxpayers provide their hard-earned dollars to government officials, they hope to receive a tangible outcome for this investment in public services. The true measure of success for these tax dollars is not how much is being spent but whether a measurable performance outcome is being achieved. This is why state and local budgets should be transformed from a list of spending to a performance agreement with taxpayers on what the expected results will be for these investments. This type of budgeting is known as performance-based budgeting.

---

[3] "Constitution," South Dakota Legislature, accessed on October 23, 2023, available at https://sdlegislature.gov/Constitution/11-14

Although many states use a variation of performance-based budgeting, Texas is the clearest example of transforming a state's actual appropriation bills into a performance agreement with taxpayers on what outcomes are expected. As noted in a 2005 United States Government Accountability Office (GAO) audit:[4]

> "In Texas, funds are appropriated by agency goals and strategies, which are defined in the agency's strategic plan. Strategies set forth actions to be taken by an agency to achieve its goals. There may be multiple strategies under one goal. Funding is provided at the strategy level . . . in Texas agencies work with legislative and executive budget staff throughout the strategic planning and budgeting processes to determine the measures they will report in the next biennial budget."

GAO further notes about the Texas performance-based budgeting process:

> "In addition to funding amounts, the legislative budget estimates and general appropriations bill also include other budget-related information, such as performance measures and targets, financing procedures, and historical summaries of previous funding requests and approved agency budgets. The Governor's Office also provides its budget proposal at the beginning of the legislative session using a similar format as the LBB . . .
>
> Texas's General Appropriation Act is structured by goals and strategies. In general, an agency will have three to five substantive strategies, sometimes referred to as 'direct strategies,' as well as one or more strategies labeled 'indirect administration' for functions shared among strategies, such as accounting, human resources, information

---

[4] "Performance Budgeting - States' Experiences Can Inform Federal Efforts," GAO, February 2005, available at https://www.gao.gov/assets/gao-05-215.pdf

technology, reporting, and overall administration in the higher executive offices . . .

Texas also includes outcome, output, and efficiency targets to show what level of performance is expected for each goal and strategy based on the appropriation level each receives."

Here is an example of what the Texas budget looks like by using this type of process:[5]

DEPARTMENT OF TRANSPORTATION
(Continued)

Client Services	2,860,414	2,872,280
Grants	1,033,369,922	571,045,116
Capital Expenditures	6,431,481,695	6,565,557,784
Total, Object-of-Expense Informational Listing	$ 18,632,354,551	$ 18,683,509,447
Estimated Allocations for Employee Benefits and Debt Service Appropriations Made Elsewhere in this Act:		
Employee Benefits		
Retirement	$ 76,797,690	$ 81,744,654
Group Insurance	212,376,192	218,578,630
Social Security	61,672,267	65,654,564
Benefits Replacement	349,500	279,251
Subtotal, Employee Benefits	$ 351,195,649	$ 366,257,099
Debt Service		
TPFA GO Bond Debt Service	$ 9,136,396	$ 7,102,641
Total, Estimated Allocations for Employee Benefits and Debt Service Appropriations Made Elsewhere in this Act	$ 360,332,045	$ 373,359,740

---

[5] "General Appropriations Act for The 2024-25 Biennium," Texas Legislature, February 2005, accessed on May 21, 2024, available at https://www.lbb.texas.gov/Documents/GAA/General_Appropriations_Act_2024_2025.pdf

1. **Performance Measure Targets.** The following is a listing of the key performance target levels for the Department of Transportation. It is the intent of the Legislature that appropriations made by this Act be utilized in the most efficient and effective manner possible to achieve the intended mission of the Department of Transportation. In order to achieve the objectives and service standards established by this Act, the Department of Transportation shall make every effort to attain the following designated key performance target levels associated with each item of appropriation.

	2024	2025
A. Goal: PROJECT DEVELOPMENT AND DELIVERY		
Outcome (Results/Impact):		
Percent of Design Projects Delivered on Time	90%	90%
Percent of Construction Projects Completed on Budget	85%	85%
Percent of Two-lane Highways 26 Feet or Wider in Paved Width	54.8%	54.9%
Percent of Construction Projects Completed on Time	65%	65%
A.1.1. Strategy: PLAN/DESIGN/MANAGE		
Output (Volume):		
Number of Construction Plans Processed for Statewide Construction Letting	765	765
Dollar Volume of Construction Contracts Awarded (Millions)	6,500	6,500
Number of Construction Contracts Awarded	765	765
B. Goal: ROUTINE SYSTEM MAINTENANCE		
Outcome (Results/Impact):		
Bridge Inventory Condition Score	88.68	88.59
Percent of Highway Pavements in Good or Better Condition	90%	90%
B.1.1. Strategy: CONTRACTED ROUTINE		

The Texas Legislative Budget Board further explains:[6]

> "As a part of the strategic planning process, agencies develop performance measures. Performance measures are quantifiable indicators of achievement. Texas uses four types of measures:

☐ Outcome—indicates the effect on a stated condition;

☐ Output—counts the services produced by an agency;

☐ Efficiency—gauges resource cost per unit of product; and

☐ Explanatory/input—provides information to help assess reported performance . . .

> Over the next two years, an agency collects data on its performance measures and reports this information quarterly to the LBB, GBPD, and other agencies. As part of the data collection process, an

[6] "Budget 101," Texas Legislature, January 2023, available at https://senate.texas.gov/_assets/srcpub/88th_Budget_101.pdf

agency must establish controls to ensure the data is properly collected and reported. Among the duties of the SAO are auditing performance measures and certifying those measures. The audit report on performance measures includes a report on the adequacy of controls in reporting data and the accuracy of agency reporting on actual performance."

Although caseloads, inflation, and population changes are important drivers of budget pressures, the fiscal conversation should always be focused on what the expected performance outcomes are for the taxpayer investments being made. By using a budgeting process that places desired performance outcomes directly into the actual appropriation bills, budget writers can help refocus the spending debate while signaling a clear expectation to agencies on what they are expected to accomplish on behalf of taxpayers.

III.   **Adopt automatic tax rebates tied to revenue triggers**

Along with providing constitutional tax increase protections, several states like Oregon and Colorado also require automatic tax rebates when revenues grow above a certain level. Here are details on how that automatic refund process works in those states.

The Oregon Department of Revenue explains:[7]

> "The Oregon surplus credit, known as the 'kicker,' is a way for state government to return some of your taxes to you when revenues are more than predicted. Every two years, the Oregon Department of Administrative Services (DAS) Office of Economic Analysis (OEA) determines whether there is a surplus and the amount to be returned to taxpayers as a kicker. If there's a surplus, the kicker may be claimed on the return as a refundable tax credit or donated to the State School Fund . . . The 1979 Oregon

---

[7] "Oregon surplus 'Kicker' credit," Oregon Department of Revenue, accessed on October 23, 2023, available at
https://www.oregon.gov/dor/programs/individuals/pages/kicker.aspx

Legislature passed the 'Two percent kicker' law, which requires the state to refund excess revenue to taxpayers when actual General Fund revenues exceed the forecast amount by more than two percent."

This has resulted in billions of dollars of tax refunds for Oregonians in 2023:[8]

"Oregon taxpayers are set to receive their biggest kicker tax rebate on record when they file their taxes next spring — a $5.6 billion refund, according to near-final forecasts issued Wednesday. That works out to $980 for the median taxpayer."

According to the Colorado Department of Revenue:[9]

"The Taxpayer's Bill of Rights (TABOR) Amendment was approved by voters in 1992. This amendment to the Constitution of the State of Colorado generally limits the amount of revenue governments in the state can retain and spend. Absent voter approval, it requires excess revenue to be refunded to taxpayers. TABOR also requires voter approval for certain tax increases. The state TABOR revenue limit is generally equal to the prior fiscal year's limit plus the rate of inflation and population growth in Colorado, subject to a voter-approved floor."

Here is an example of what the Colorado tax refund looked like in 2023:[10]

---

[8] "Oregon taxpayers set to receive record $5.6 billion kicker; here's what you can expect,' The Oregonian, August 2023, available at
https://www.oregonlive.com/business/2023/08/oregon-taxpayers-set-to-receive-record-56-billion-kicker-heres-what-you-can-expect.html
[9] "Taxpayer's Bill of Rights (TABOR) Information," Colorado Department of Revenue, accessed on October 23, 2023, available at https://tax.colorado.gov/TABOR
[10] "Why are TABOR refunds so huge lately? And will they stay that way?," CPR News, September 2023, available at https://www.cpr.org/2023/09/21/colorado-why-are-tabor-refunds-so-huge-lately/

"Colorado is set to pay out more than $3.5 billion in TABOR refunds next spring — one of the largest paybacks that the state has ever had to return to taxpayers. In fact, the state is in the middle of what could be a record-busting string of revenue years. For the first time ever, the state government could be forced to pay refunds for six straight years, stretching from 2022 through 2027 or longer. Those refunds are expected to average more than $2 billion per year."

Authorizing automatic tax rebate triggers based on revenue growth, like what occurs in Oregon and Colorado, will help policymakers avoid the temptation of overheating a state budget and increasing the pressure for future tax increases.

IV.   Use revenue triggers to reduce income tax rates

Over the past few years, lawmakers in Idaho and Montana have been working on income tax reform by reducing rates. The tax reduction action in both states follow a national trend. One of the only states not following the trend happens to be neighboring Washington, providing a golden opportunity for policymakers in Idaho and Montana to take advantage of an extraordinary policy shift and solidify state competitiveness for years to come.

Comparing income tax rates

Income tax rates vary significantly. Wyoming and Nevada do not levy income taxes, while Washington state added a new capital gains income tax in 2023. California has the highest income tax rates in the country. Colorado and Utah both have income taxes, but they have been gradually reduced.

While the reductions and focus on rates in Idaho and Montana are welcome, both states risk falling behind their neighbors if they don't take further action. Furthermore, states across the country with personal income taxes have sought to lower the burden.

Income tax rates, by state

As of April 2024

State	Rate	State	Rate
California	13.3%	Alabama	5.0%
Hawaii	11.0%	Illinois	4.95%
New York	10.9%	Missouri	4.80%
New Jersey	10.75%	Oklahoma	4.75%
District of Columbia	10.75%	Mississippi	4.70%
Minnesota	9.85%	Utah	4.65%
Oregon	9.9%	Arkansas	4.40%
Massachusetts	9.0%	Colorado	4.40%
Vermont	8.75%	Louisiana	4.25%
Washington	7.00%	Michigan	4.25%
Wisconsin	7.65%	Kentucky	4.0%
Connecticut	6.99%	Ohio	3.5%
Delaware	6.60%	Pennsylvania	3.07%
South Carolina	6.4%	Indiana	3.05%
Rhode Island	5.99%	New Hampshire	3.0%
Montana	5.90%	North Dakota	2.5%
New Mexico	5.90%	Arizona	2.5%
Nebraska	5.84%	Tennessee	0%
Virginia	5.75%	Nevada	0%
Maryland	5.75%	Wyoming	0%
Kansas	5.70%	Alaska	0%
Iowa	5.70%	South Dakota	0%
Idaho	5.69%	Florida	0%
Georgia	5.49%	Texas	0%

Tying sustained revenue growth to rate reductions

So how can lawmakers ensure the tax burden remains low, and a state is not over-collecting? One option is to tie the state's income tax rate to excess revenue via a trigger. As the Tax Foundation reports:[11]

> "When North Carolina legislators committed to comprehensive tax reform in 2013, they broadened tax bases and eliminated exemptions to fund rate reductions—but then turned to 'tax triggers' to implement a schedule of further rate cuts, as revenue permitted, in subsequent years. Seeking a lower individual income tax rate, Massachusetts policymakers opted for a gradual phase-in of rate cuts, proceeding only when revenue growth was more than sufficient to absorb the rate change."

By using automatic triggers, there would be no need for special sessions of the legislature or one-time tax rebate checks that show the government has over-collected. The reduction would happen automatically.

Use revenue triggers to buy down income tax rates
Idaho example, wherein .1% of income tax equals $40 million in revenue

State has $120 million in excess, sustained revenue, equaling .3% of state income tax rate

Rate is automatically reduced from 5.695% to 5.395%

The exact revenue percentage over expectations, the period of time required to make sure it is consistent, and the corresponding income tax rate reduction would all need to be set by lawmakers. Adopting this type of policy would send a

---

[11] 8 Tax Foundation, Designing tax triggers: lessons from the states, available at https://taxfoundation.org/designing-tax-triggerslessons-states/?fbclid=IwAR2h9kD4V6mkBQQ2cbxl3RU0ZJl574Tf-fSYLuePYGUZMAvzlRuDOMpaWRI

clear message that Idaho and Montana will continue to lower the income tax burden it is placing on families and businesses. And the more the economy booms, the lower the rate.

As the Tax Foundation notes, "tax triggers can help ensure revenue stability and limit the uncertainty associated with changes to the tax code while providing an efficient way for states to dedicate some portion of revenue growth to tax relief."

How rate reductions could help the economy and state credit ratings

Economic analyses have found that tax cuts – specifically income tax cuts – are likely to immediately boost gross domestic product (GDP). Karel Mertens and Morten Ravn with the American Economic Review found that the progressivity of an income tax hurts economic growth. Idaho and Montana lawmakers have already addressed this issue by flattening the state's income tax rate.[12] But Mertens and Ravn further found "a 1 percentage point cut in the average personal income tax rate raises real GDP per capita by 1.4 percent in the first quarter and by up to 1.8 percent after three quarters."

Meantime, it is worth noting that states that rely heavily on income taxes to support government revenue can find themselves on a roller coaster ride during inevitable economic downturns. This is because layoffs can crash a state's income tax revenue, while sales taxes are more likely to be reliable.

This is confirmed by credit agencies across the country, including Standard and Poor's (S&P), which says, "sales tax-

---

[12] 4 Tax Foundation, Evidence of Taxes and Growth, 2012, available at https://taxfoundation.org/what-evidence-taxes-andgrowth/

based revenue structure... has demonstrated less sensitivity to economic cycles than income tax-reliant states."[13]

While no revenue source is immune to economic waves, graduated and capital gains income taxes are the most volatile taxes.[14]

Rarely do policymakers get such an enormous opportunity to take advantage of surging tax revenues and the economic environment to lower the tax burden in their states and bring more stability to government revenues. With a revenue trigger, the more the state has in surplus, the lower the tax rate will go.

As the Tax Foundation points out, "well-designed triggers limit the volatility and unpredictability associated with any change to revenue codes and can be a valuable tool for states seeking to balance the economic impetus for tax reform with a governmental need for revenue predictability."

V. Move local tax levies and bonds to the November general election

Unfortunately, many elections suffer from low voter turnout, leaving government requests to voters for increased tax collections in the hands of a relatively small number of citizens. This is especially true for 'special elections' that are held throughout the year separately from the November general election when few voters are paying attention.

To counter the few from imposing a long-term tax obligation on the community without broad consensus, several states require supermajority votes for certain types of tax increases.

---

[13] 5 S&P Global Ratings, State of Washington Appropriations, General Obligation, July 11, 2022, available at https://www.tre.wa.gov/wp-content/uploads/2023AT-SP-2022.07.11-Report.pdf

[14] Tax Foundation, Income taxes are more volatile than sales taxes during an economic contraction, by Jared Walczak, March 17, 2020, available at https://taxfoundation.org/income-taxes-are-more-volatile-than-sales-taxes-during-recession/

There are many good reasons to require a supermajority, even with voter approval, for bonds such as those for schools. Unlike normal levies, these bond obligations can extend for many years and the taxes can't be repealed or reduced until that obligation is met. Most other tax levies can be changed or repealed at any time. This prevents tying the hands of future policymakers so they can respond to changing economic conditions.

The main exception to this flexibility, however, is for taxes pledged to bonds (long-term contractual obligations). Realizing the different nature of taxes for bonds versus normal operating expenses and wanting to prevent a small number of voters from imposing this type of long-term tax burden on a community, many constitutions across the country require these bond votes to secure a broad consensus.

Although several states require a 3/5 vote for school bonds (including neighboring Washington), Idaho is one of the few in the country with an exceptionally high requirement to secure a 2/3 vote of the people.

Moving to a 3/5 vote requirement for school bonds, if the election is required to be held at the November general for maximum voter turnout and involvement, is a discussion worth having. What shouldn't happen is allowing 'special elections' with low voter turnout to increase the long-term tax obligation of a community.

Voter turnout by state
2008-2022

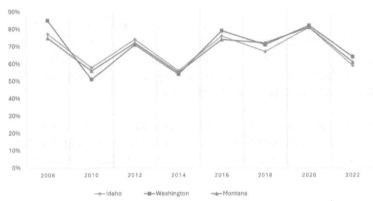

Idaho ● Washington ▪ Montana ▲

POLICY MANUAL

One possible idea would be to give school districts a choice. They could use a special election and need to meet a 2/3 vote, or they could place the bond tax levy on the November general election and need to secure a 3/5 vote. It is false to say this will only make tax increases easier. In fact, in a higher turnout election, you'll have to convince more voters that the tax increase is warranted. The goal is to allow the full voice of the community to be heard by making these tax decisions at the elections with the highest voter turnout.

Long-term tax obligations should never be easy to impose, but Idaho's current 2/3 vote requirement for school bonds, even with voter approval, is an exceedingly high threshold that should be reconsidered. By moving all tax levies to the November general election while still requiring a 3/5 vote for bonds, policymakers can encourage a robust tax discussion in the community to occur and secure a broad consensus before a long-term tax obligation is imposed.

As for normal operating levies that only need to meet a majority threshold, those too should be moved to the November general election. There is never a good argument

17

to use a low-turnout election to ask the community to increase taxes on families and businesses.

VI.   Idaho's controversial grocery tax

Idaho is one of only 13 states that still taxes groceries, and the Gem State has one of the highest rates at a full 6% (the state's current sales tax). Montana doesn't have a sales tax, while Wyoming exempts food and Washington does not attach its sales tax to most grocery items.

In Utah, residents are currently charged 3% on groceries statewide, but lawmakers have proposed eliminating the state portion of the tax (currently 1.75%) via a ballot measure in November of 2024.

Grocery tax rates, by state
The Tax Foundation

State	Ordinary Rate	Grocery Rate	Offset or Rebate?
Alabama	4%	4%	
Arkansas	6.5%	0.125%	
Hawaii	4%	4%	x
Idaho	6%	6%	x
Illinois	6.25%	1%	
Kansas	6.50%	6.5%	x
Mississippi	7%	7%	
Missouri	4.225%	1.225%	
Oklahoma	4.5%	4.5%	x
South Dakota	4.5%	4.5%	
Tennessee	7.0%	4.0%	
Utah	4.85%	1.75%	x
Virginia	5.3%	2.50%	

Taxing food is controversial. Idaho offers a yearly rebate of $100-$120 to residents – a number that appears smaller as inflation roars.

In 2017, then Idaho Lt. Governor Brad Little urged Governor Butch Otter to sign a proposed repeal of the state's grocery tax.[15] Other candidates and political leaders have called for a

---

[15] Little: Repeal the Idaho sales tax on groceries, Associated Press, April 3, 2017, available at https://apnews.com/general-news-ac30e2b295cd4b738a4baa7d24a706ff

similar reduction or repeal, wrongly assuming that it would have a progressive effect. Instead of repealing or exempting the tax for all, grocery tax credits or rebates offer the poorest households better savings.

Research from the Tax Foundation concludes[16]:

> "Grocery exemptions are a middle -income, not a low - income, benefit—and middle earners can be more efficiently made whole through grocery tax credits. Higher earning households purchase not only more, but higher qualities of, groceries. Low-income households, in fact, are more likely to purchase taxable substitutes to what states classify as groceries, a category that traditionally only covers unprepared foods. The result is that a household in the fifth decile spends almost 70 percent more than a household in the first decile, and a household in the top decile spends over three times as much as a household in the lowest.

The distributional effects of grocery taxation diverge sharply from most policymakers' expectations, which has dramatic ramifications for this ongoing debate and suggests better ways to achieve policymakers' desired aims."

---

[16] The surprising regressivity of grocery tax exemptions, by Jared Walczak, Tax Foundation, April 2022, available at https://files.taxfoundation.org/20220412163431/The-Surprising-Regressivity-of-Grocery-Tax-Exemptions.pdf

Grocery expenditures as a percentage of lowest income decile's expenditures

The Tax Foundation

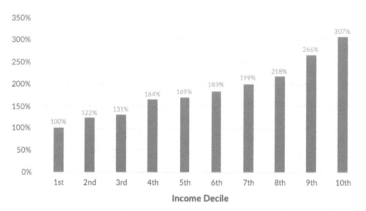

Sales taxes are more stable and pro-growth than other forms of taxation – especially income taxes. Policymakers can better serve citizens by adopting higher yearly grocery tax rebates and focus remaining excess revenue on cutting income taxes.

VII. Sugary drink taxes are poor public policy

Policymakers have various tax levers available, but one they should avoid pulling is a tax specifically on sugary beverages.

These taxes often come with promises to decrease sugar consumption and raise revenue for popular programs. These goals are counterintuitive. If soda taxes were successful in deterring consumption, the revenue stream for popular programs would decrease.

Research has been mixed. In Seattle, where in 2018 city leaders adopted a 1.75 cents per fluid ounce sugary beverage tax, there was little evidence of impact. In fact, research conducted by the city showed that, while consumption of beverages did decline, it declined more in neighboring cities which did not have a sugary beverage tax.[17]

Peer-reviewed research on the Seattle beverage tax also showed a significant increase in beer purchases following implementation, suggesting alternative purchases were not necessarily healthy.[18] Policymakers are essentially using taxes to play sugar whack-a-mole.

Additional data on Philadelphia's sugary drink tax shows a reduction in sugar drink consumption, but an increase in the purchases of sugary foods. Researchers simply concluded "the policy can be undermined by consumers changing their sources of sugar."[19]

Sugary drink taxes are very regressive. Lower income adults consume 40% more sugary drinks each day than higher income adults. Lower income children consumer 2.5 times as many sugary drinks than higher income children.[20] This means low income households are hit much harder by any sugary beverage tax.

VIII.   **Adopt a 30-day work requirement for income tax liability**

As a result of the COVID-19 lockdowns, remote work has been surging. According to the United States Census Bureau, the number and percent of home-based workers more than tripled between 2019 and 2021, from 5.7% (roughly 9 million workers) to 17.9% (about 28 million workers).[21]

---

[17] Twelve month report: Store Audits and Child Cohort, The Evaluation of Seattle's sweetened beverage tax, March 2020, conducted by the City of Seattle, available at https://www.documentcloud.org/documents/6838848-12-Month-SBT-Report-Final.html

[18] Impact of the Seattle Sweetened Beverage Tax on substitution to alcoholic beverages, January 18, 2022, University of Illinois, available at https://journals.plos.org/plosone/article?id=10.1371/journal.pone.0262578#references

[19] National Library of Medicine, The effect of soda taxes beyond beverages in Philadelphia, August 2022, available at https://www.ncbi.nlm.nih.gov/pmc/articles/PMC9804786/

[20] Urban Institute, The pros and cons of taxing sweetened beverages based on sugar, The Urban Institute, December 2016, available at https://www.urban.org/sites/default/files/publication/86541/2001024-the-pros-and-cons-of-taxing-sweetened-beverages-based-on-sugar-content.pdf

[21] "The Number of People Primarily Working From Home Tripled Between 2019 and 2021," U.S. Census Bureau, September 15, 2022, available at

Consequently, this trend towards remote work needs the proper policy actions by policymakers to allow these employees to both thrive in their positions and incentivize them to work in the state. As remote-based companies grow, they need to have the assurance that the states their employees reside in are well suited for their sector of work.

There is a great administrative advantage for employers to have the option to choose from job candidates all around the country without experiencing hesitations around state's tax policies. One of the areas of policy involved is an income tax obligation or withholding threshold.

This is the limit that employees must exceed in a state before they are either liable to pay the state income tax, or employers are required to withhold income taxes on the employees' behalf. Around the country, states have been looking at ways to increase this threshold to make their state attractive for remote and nonresident employees to work out of. Idaho should follow suit.

As it stands in Idaho, a nonresident employee must make $1,000 while in Idaho, to have their employer withhold their income tax for the state. While this policy is mainly associated with remote workers, it also affects those who engage in frequent business travel, and those who desire to work in a hybrid model in a different state.

Example from Montana

Several states are acting to reform their nonresident income tax thresholds. In May of 2023, Montana passed a 30-day threshold for income tax liability. HB 447 states that:[22]

> "Compensation that is received by a nonresident for employment duties performed in this state, is

https://www.census.gov/newsroom/press-releases/2022/people-working-from-home.html

[22] "HB 447- 2023," Montana Legislature, accessed on May 21, 2024, available at https://leg.mt.gov/bills/2023/billhtml/HB0447.htm

excluded from Montana source income if: The nonresident is present in this state to perform employment duties for not more than 30 days during the tax year in which the compensation is received, where presence in this state for any part of a day constitutes presence."

While the issue of income tax relating to nonresident workers is treated differently throughout the country, Idaho should consider moving to a 30-day income tax obligation threshold. The state needs to both encourage remote and nonresident workers to operate in Idaho and ensure that employees aren't taking advantage of a tax loophole.

A 30-day threshold would accomplish both. A wage threshold proves to be very complicated in the case of an employer with employees in multiple states. The employer must take all the specific wage thresholds into consideration while making hires and sending employees to other states for meetings, conferences, and other forms of business engagement.

A wage threshold also disincentives entrepreneurs from organizing events like business conferences. If the organizers know they will be obligated to pay the income tax within a given state if they exceed a certain compensation level, they will simply relocate to a state where they wouldn't be penalized in.

The 30-day mark provides adequate time for nonresidents to collaborate with residents while participating in the local economy. The current threshold standard in Idaho is lacking compared to the 30-day-specific direction that states like Montana are following.

IX.   **End taxpayer subsidies to government unions**

For many people, labor unions conjure up images of hard hats and factory floors. But such notions are increasingly out-of-date. The largest and most influential labor unions in America today represent government employees. Government unions have immense incentives to use electoral politics to capture control of government. Unlike their counterparts in private industry, government unions "have the ability, in a sense, to elect our own boss," as New York union leader Victor Gotbaum infamously proclaimed in 1975.[23]

This type of political activity should not be subsidized by taxpayers. There's nothing wrong with a private membership organization supporting whatever cause, candidate or party it likes, so long as it does so with its own funds. But representative government is often about balancing competing interests and, when a private interest co-opts the government itself, it can use the power of the state to quash competing voices.

This type of political phenomenon is most accurately seen in the activities of government teachers' unions. While teachers and public school employees are certainly *one* interest group with a valid stake in the operation of government schools, the interests of students, families and taxpayers matter, too.

Unfortunately, when school boards allow teachers' unions to benefit from public funds, facilities, and resources, they artificially amplify union influence and warp democratic processes. Taxpayers already fund the management side of the bargaining table; they shouldn't also have to pick up the tab for union bargaining against their interests and advocacy for controversial political views.

State lawmakers can and should protect taxpayers and level the playing field by prohibiting direct government funding for teachers' unions, requiring unions to reimburse school districts for the cost of teachers' paid union leave, providing that teachers unions get no more access to or use of school facilities than any other civic group, and ending government collection of union dues via payroll deduction.

---

[23] "Captive Politicians," New York Times, July 9, 1975, available at https://www.nytimes.com/1975/07/09/archives/captive-politicians.html

X.   Support efforts to require a federal balanced budget amendment

Every U.S. state except for Vermont has a requirement to pass a balanced budget. This important fiscal requirement is essential to maintaining fiscal health and a strong economic outlook. Unfortunately, there is no requirement for Congress to adopt a balanced budget. As a result, it is no surprise that the nation's fiscal outlook is teetering on the brink.

According to the Congressional Budget Office:[24]

> "Federal debt held by the public increases each year in CBO's projections, swelling to an all-time record of 116 percent of GDP in 2034. In the two decades that follow, growing deficits cause debt to soar to 172 percent of GDP by 2054."

Projected federal debt
Congressional Budget Office

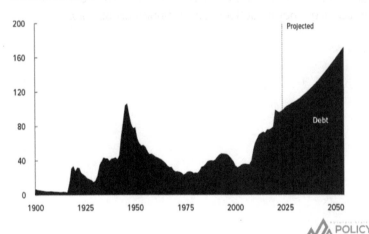

---

24 "The Budget and Economic Outlook: 2024 to 2034," CBO, February 2024, available at
https://www.cbo.gov/publication/59946

XI.   **Support efforts to call a fiscally focused Convention of the states**

With Congress unwilling to take the necessary steps to budget responsibly, several states are now exercising their rights under the U.S. Constitution to initiate an Article V convention to put forward constitutional amendments to require federal fiscal discipline.

Some have expressed concern that a convention of the states could lead to a runaway process that drastically alters the current U.S. Constitution. One important thing to keep in mind about this fear is that any amendments advanced by this process would still have to be ratified by 3/4 of the states. It is doubtful that anything without broad public support would be enacted by 38 states with this safeguard.

It is clear that Congress is not capable of enacting the reforms needed to change the course of runaway federal spending. That duty now falls on the states to secure the nation's economic outlook for continued prosperity.

I.   **Create a Tax Transparency website**

To be fully engaged in our governance, citizens need to be
able to evaluate the level and value of service they receive for
the taxes they pay. One of the ways to do this is with budget
transparency resources like Transparent Idaho[1] and
Washington State Fiscal Information.[2] Spending details,
however, are only part of the equation. Meaningful
transparency on the amount of taxes we pay and to whom is
often the missing component.

Consider just how many taxing districts (entities with the
authority to impose taxes) there are in each of the Mountain
States:

Total number of taxing districts

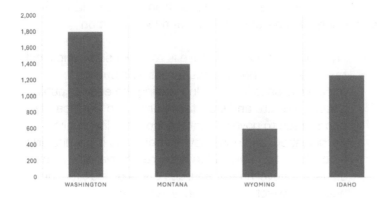

This means the typical home and business in these states
could be subject to numerous taxing districts at the same
time. The ability to hold the appropriate level of government

---

[1] "Transparent Idaho," available at https://transparent.idaho.gov/
[2] "Washington State Fiscal Information," available at https://fiscal.wa.gov/

accountable for that tax burden means knowing how much of the total tax bill they are responsible for and if the cost is worth the level and quality of service provided.

Now imagine if you could go to a tax transparency website and enter your home or business address to quickly see all the taxing districts you are subject to, at what rates, and perhaps be provided an educational calculator on your total estimated tax liability based on where you live.

Example from Washington State

Lawmakers in Washington State in 2024 adopted a budget proviso "to develop an implementation plan for an online searchable database of all taxes and tax rates in the state for each taxing district."[3]

The Washington State tax transparency website budget proviso is modeled after the requirements from a bipartisan 2023 bill. Here is the intent section from that bill: SB 5158 - Concerning transparency in state and local taxation:[4]

> "The intent of the legislature is to make state and local tax revenue as open, transparent, and publicly accessible as is feasible. Increasing the ease of public access to state and local tax information significantly contributes to governmental accountability, public participation, and open government; this is particularly true when the information is currently available from disparate government sources but is difficult for the public to collect and efficiently aggregate."

U.S. Supreme Court Justice Oliver Wendell Holmes, Jr, once noted, "Taxes are the price we pay for a civilized society."

---

[3] "Senate Bill 5187 - 2023," Washington state Legislature, available at https://lawfilesext.leg.wa.gov/biennium/2023-24/Pdf/Bills/Session%20Laws/Senate/5187-S.SL.pdf?q=20231012130316
[4] "Senate Bill 5158 – 2023," Washington state Legislature, available at https://app.leg.wa.gov/billsummary?BillNumber=5158&Initiative=false&Year=2023

Civilization, however, need not be shrouded in the mystery of compounding tax districts without meaningful transparency. Policymakers in the Mountain States should remove the mystery surrounding taxation by adopting a tax transparency website.

II. Adopt Truth in Taxation to improve accountability for property taxes

Property taxes are an important part of the tax base for school districts, local governments, and many states. Though based on a relatively straightforward calculation, they are among the least understood taxes by taxpayers. Although there are variations in each state, the general formula for property taxes is the value of the property multiplied by the tax rate.

When considering their property tax burden, too often taxpayers focus on assessed values instead of the spending decisions made by government officials. With record property tax assessment increases occurring in states like Idaho, Montana, and Wyoming, homeowners are concerned about the potential impact on their property tax bills. First, it is important for taxpayers to know that assessments are just a part of the calculation. The main driver of property taxes is spending increases approved by policymakers and voters themselves through levies.

This is why efforts to restrict property assessments are often misplaced and lead to other problems.[5] The better way to control property tax increases is on the spending side and/or with levy restrictions. One way to help bring greater transparency to the fact spending is the main cause of property tax increases is with a reform called Truth in Taxation.

---

[5] "A History of Property Tax in Utah," Utah Legislature, September 2010, available at https://le.utah.gov/lrgc/briefings/BriefingPaperPropertyTaxHistorySept2010.pdf

Utah's Truth in Taxation Example

To bring more transparency to property tax increases, Utah was the first to adopt Truth in Taxation in 1985.

Here is how the Utah Legislature describes the state's Truth in Taxation law:[6]

> "The basic concept of the system is that taxing entities may only budget the same amount of property tax each year, unless they have 'new growth' (not just change in value on existing properties) or go through a very public process of notifying the public and holding a public hearing on the proposed revenue increase. To achieve this, as taxable values change, the tax rate automatically adjusts to provide a constant amount of revenue. When values increase, the tax rate adjusts down to provide the taxing entity the same amount of revenue as it received in the prior year. When values decrease, the tax rate adjusts up to provide the same amount of revenue."

Utah's Property Tax Division further explains:[7]

> "Property Tax increases require a Truth in Taxation process of public disclosure. Taxing entities are required to follow a series of date specific steps, including notification to the county, newspaper advertisements, parcel specific notices, and a public hearing, before adopting a property tax rate above a calculated certified tax rate. The timeline is different for a fiscal year taxing entity (budget cycle July 1 to June 30) and a calendar year entity (budget cycle Jan 1 to Dec 31)."

---

[6] "A History of Property Tax in Utah," Utah Legislature, September 2010, available at https://le.utah.gov/lrgc/briefings/BriefingPaperPropertyTaxHistorySept2010.pdf
[7] "Tax Increase Requirements," Utah Property Tax Division, accessed on September 2023, available at https://propertytax.utah.gov/tax-increases/

Assessment Type	2023 Market Value	COMPARE 2022 Market Value	RIGHT TO APPEAL
FULL MARKET VALUE	$532,200	$548,900	If you believe the assessed value of your property is incorrect, you may begin the appeal process by filing an Appeal Form with the County Auditor by 09/15/23. Visit slco.org/property-tax/
RESIDENT EXEMPTION REDUCTION	<239,490>	<247,005>	
TOTAL TAXABLE VALUE	$292,710	$301,895	

For detailed property valuation information visit slco.org/assessor/

NOTICE OF TAX CHANGES

TAXING ENTITY	2023 IF TAX INCREASE APPROVED Rate	Tax	2023 IF NO BUDGET CHANGE Rate	Tax	2023 CHANGE IF INCREASE APPROVED Tax	%	2022 Rate	Tax	RIGHT TO BE HEARD A public meeting will be held Date/Time/Place
CANYONS SCHOOL DISTRICT	.004231	1,238.46	.004231	1,238.46			.004336	1,309.02	
STATE BASIC SCHOOL LEVY	.001406	411.55	.001406	411.55			.001652	498.73	
UT CHARTER SCHOOL-CANYONS	.000068	19.90	.000068	19.90			.000065	19.62	
SALT LAKE COUNTY	.001394	408.03	.001394	408.03			.001469	440.45	
SANDY CITY	.001057	309.39	.000920	269.29	$40.10	15%	.000942	284.39	08/22/23,06:00PM 10006 S Centennial Pkwy
SL COUNTY LIBRARY	.000477	139.62	.000381	111.52	$28.10	25%	.000386	116.53	HEARING HELD DEC '22
SO SL VALLEY MOSQUITO	.000009	2.63	.000009	2.63			.000009	2.72	
METRO WATER SANDY	.000216	63.23	.000216	63.23			.000221	66.72	
COTTONWOOD IMPROVEMENT	.000176	51.52	.000118	34.54	$16.98	49%	.000119	35.93	HEARING HELD NOV 14
ALTA CANYON REC SPCL SVCE	.000113	33.08	.000113	33.08			.000114	34.42	
CENTRAL UT WATER CONSERV	.000400	117.08	.000387	113.29	$3.80	3%	.000400	120.76	08/21/23,06:00PM 1426 E 750 N Bldg 2 Orem
MULTI COUNTY ASSESS/COLL	.000015	4.39	.000015	4.39			.000015	4.63	
COUNTY ASSESS/COLL LEVY	.000155	45.38	.000155	45.38			.000160	48.30	
TOTAL	.009717	2,844.26	.009413	2,755.28			.009878	2,982.12	

VALUES DO NOT INCLUDE TAX RELIEF, DELINQUENT TAXES, PERSONAL PROPERTY TAXES, OR SPECIAL ASSESSMENTS. APPLY FOR TAX RELIEF BY SEPTEMBER 1 AT SLCO.ORG/TREASURER/TAX-RELIEF/ THIS IS NOT A BILL. DO NOT PAY.

Along with Utah, Truth in Taxation currently exists in Iowa, Kansas, Nebraska, and Tennessee.

Montana Governor Greg Gianforte succinctly explained the need for policymakers to focus on property tax transparency when he said in 2023:[8]

> "To ease the property tax burden, we must reform our system and bring greater transparency, accountability, and responsibility to local spending."

Even though Idaho doesn't have a statewide property tax and the legislature recently enacted property tax rebates to help with the local tax burden, Truth in Taxation is still needed to

---

[8] "Delivering income and property tax relief for Montanans," Independent Record, July 2023, available at https://helenair.com/opinion/column/greg-gianforte-delivering-income-and-property-tax-relief-for-montanans/article_09191952-2d73-11ee-9d53-536912f93301.html

help empower taxpayers to better engage and understand their property tax burden and the connection to spending.[9]

With the cry for property tax reform getting louder, policymakers in the Mountain States should focus their efforts on improving transparency and voter engagement with Truth in Taxation.

III.   **Use a taxpayer receipt to help provide a snapshot of government spending**

We're all familiar with the shopping experience of seeing the total amount we owe ring up on the register and then being provided with an itemized receipt showing what we purchased. This simple sheet of paper helps us remember and understand where our shopping dollars went. Now imagine if you were provided with a taxpayer receipt providing the same information for your tax dollars and how it relates to government spending.

Utah is doing just this. Adopted by lawmakers in 2013, HB 129 required the Office of Legislative Fiscal Office:[10]

"To develop a taxpayer receipt: (i) available to taxpayers through a website; and (ii) that allows a taxpayer to view on the website an estimate of how the taxpayer's tax dollars are expended for government purposes; and to publish or provide other information on taxation and government expenditures that may be accessed by the public."

VIDEO: The taxpayer receipt

---

[9] "Idaho property tax relief going forward after all," Mountain States Policy Center, March 2023, available at https://www.mountainstatespolicy.org/idaho-property-tax-relief-going-forward-after-all

[10] "H.B. 129 Amendments to Powers, Functions, and Duties of Office of Legislative Fiscal Analyst – 2013," Utah Legislature, available at https://le.utah.gov/~2013/bills/static/hb0129.html

Utah's taxpayer receipt allows users to see what their tax dollars buy by an individual providing information on household size, income, amount of home value or rent, and type of cars and miles driven.[11] The taxpayer receipt site notes:

> "Your data is not stored or sent to any government entity. Results are illustrative of a typical full-year Utah resident with similar circumstance. Only State of Utah imposed taxes. Does not include local sales or property taxes or federal fuel or income taxes. Does not include fines, fees, or other taxes and charges paid to state government."

Here is an example of what the Utah taxpayer receipt looks like by using these data points: A family of four, with $80,000 in income, a home valued at $300,000, and two midsized cars driven for a combined 40,000 miles a year.

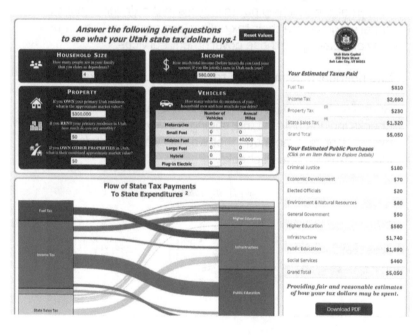

---

[11] "Taxpayer Receipt," Utah Legislature, accessed on May 22, 2024, available at https://le.utah.gov/lfa/taxpayerreceipt.html

According to the Utah taxpayer receipt, our sample family would owe $810 in fuel taxes, pay $2,690 in income taxes, $230 in state property taxes, and $1,320 in sales taxes for a total state tax liability of $5,050.

The estimated use for these tax dollars would be for the following: $180 for criminal justice, $70 for economic development, $20 for elected officials, $80 for environmental and natural resources, $50 for general government, $560 for higher education, $1,740 for infrastructure, $1,890 for public education, and $480 for social services ($5,050 in state spending).

Users of the Utah taxpayer receipt site are also able to drill down further on the data for additional information.

By combining a taxpayer receipt with a tax transparency website and state budget transparency resources, policymakers can help put taxpayers in the driver's seat to understand where their tax dollars are going and how much they are paying for those government services.

IV.   End political messaging on taxpayer refund checks

Receiving a refund for overpaid taxes is good. Having those checks include political messaging, however, is not. For example, here is language that was previously included on Idaho taxpayer refund checks.

STATE OF IDAHO

INVOICE NO./ACCOUNT NO.	DESCRIPTION	AMOUNT
0047486510	12/21 IND INCOME TAX	28.00

YOU CAN MAKE A DIFFERENCE!
BECOME A PART OF A GROUP OF DEDICATED PEOPLE WORKING TOGETHER TO SAVE OUR CHILDREN FROM THE RAVAGES OF METHAMPHETAMINES. GET INVOLVED WITH THE IDAHO METH PROJECT AND MAKE A DIFFERENCE IN THE FIGHT AGAINST METHAMPHETAMINE IN YOUR COMMUNITY-IN OUR STATE. TO DONATE BY MAIL, SEND YOUR TAX-DEDUCTIBLE CONTRIBUTION BY CHECK OR MONEY ORDER TO:
IDAHO METH PROJECT
PO BOX 738
BOISE, IDAHO 83701-0738

While this may be a worthwhile project, including this type of unrelated language on a taxpayer refund check is an example of the government unduly tipping the scales and should be avoided. HB 618, passed by the Idaho legislature in 2024, will stop this practice from occurring in the future for Idaho.[12]

From the text of HB 618:

> "Except for the state controller as the issuing officer, neither the name of any elected public official, nor any electioneering message shall appear on any warrant, including in any remittance advice or remittance memo, unless acting as an endorser or otherwise necessary for the proper execution of a warrant. For the purposes of this subsection, 'electioneering message' shall include statements regarding, expressing support for, or soliciting support for any government program or initiative or non-profit corporation, including any program or initiative of a nonprofit corporation."

Other states should follow the good example set by this new Idaho law. Consider the 2024 controversy in Washington state, where the Attorney General's office sent out $40 million worth of checks in the amounts of $50 and $120 to state residents considered 'low-income.' The money was derived from a lawsuit settlement against chicken and tune companies that had engaged in price-fixing.

The biggest complaint among critics of the checks, which were signed by the Attorney General, was that they included a personal message touting his office's successes while he was actively campaigning to become the state's next Governor.

Government officials should be commended for prioritizing tax refund checks when taxpayers overpay. The refund checks speak for themselves, however, without turning them into a government-funded political advertisement. Thanks to the action of Idaho lawmakers this session, taxpayer refund checks will no longer include political messages. Other states should follow Idaho's lead.

---

[12] 2024 Idaho Legislative Session, House Bill 618, available at
https://legislature.idaho.gov/sessioninfo/2024/legislation/H0618/

V.   Prevent overcollection for school district bond payments

If you take out a mortgage, you typically know what your payment is going to be each month, and from year to year. But if you approve a school bond in Idaho, you may only get a range.

That's because Idaho code 33-802A allows for school districts to collect up to 21 months' worth of payments in a 12 month period. This can be an excellent tool for paying off debt more quickly. But does that happen? And is it what taxpayers approved?

Consider the language used to describe recent school bonds:

Middleton School District - *"Principal not to exceed $59,435,000, to be paid off within 20 years; anticipated interest rate is 3.77% per annum."*

Vallivue School District - *"Principal not to exceed $55 million, to be paid off within 20 years; anticipated interest rate is 3.78% per annum."*

A school district in Idaho Falls was recently able to pay off its 20-year bond in just 12 years. Again, this might seem like a good thing. But it was not necessarily what voters approved. And it also allows school districts to pass more bonds in a shorter period.

Reforming this process is an important step in increasing confidence in elections and providing more transparency for taxpayers when considering school construction bonds.

I. **Provide at least three day notice of bills scheduled for a public hearing**

To help maximize public involvement in their governance, state lawmakers should amend their rules to require at least three day public notice of the bills to be heard at public hearings.

Providing advance notice of bills scheduled for public hearings is a standard practice among states. This will help provide busy citizens with the time needed to adjust schedules if they wish to provide comments on pending legislation.

VIDEO: The need for a rule of three

Examples from Washington and Montana

Here are examples of legislative rules requiring advance notice of bills scheduled for public hearings.

☐ Washington five day notice: "1. At least five days' notice shall be given of all public hearings held by any committee other than the rules committee. Such notice shall contain the date, time and place of such hearing together with the title and number of each bill, or identification of the subject matter, to be considered at such hearing. By a majority vote of the committee members present at any committee meeting such notice may be dispensed with. The reason for such action shall be set forth in a written statement preserved in the records of the meeting. 2. No committee may hold a public hearing during a regular or extraordinary session on a proposal identified as a draft unless the draft has been made available to the public at least twenty-four hours prior to the hearing. This rule does not apply during the five days prior to any cutoff established by concurrent resolution, nor does it apply to any measure exempted from the resolution."[1]

☐ Montana three day notice: "Notice of a committee hearing must be made by posting the date, time, and subject of the hearing online and in a conspicuous public place not less than three legislative days in advance of the hearing."[2]

Several state constitutions also require the text of bills to be publicly available for several days to avoid quick passage at the end of session without the opportunity for public involvement. Examples include:

☐ Michigan constitution: "No bill shall be passed or become a law at any regular session of the legislature until it has been printed or reproduced and in the possession of each house for at least five days."[3]

☐ Washington constitution: "No bill shall be considered in either house unless the time of its introduction shall have been at least ten days before the final adjournment of the legislature, unless the legislature shall otherwise direct by a vote of two-thirds of all the members elected to each house, said vote to be taken by yeas and nays and entered upon the journal, or unless the same be at a special session."[4]

---

[1] "2023-24 Legislative Manual," Washington State Legislature, accessed on May 21, 2024, available at
https://leg.wa.gov/LIC/Documents/EducationAndInformation/39834_Legislative%20Man ual%20-%20Red%20Book%202023_WEB.pdf
[2] "Rules of the Montana Legislature," Montanan Legislature, adopted January 2023, available at https://leg.mt.gov/content/Sessions/68th/2023-Rules.pdf
[3] "Michigan Constitution," Michigan Legislature, accessed on May 21, 2024, available at https://www.legislature.mi.gov/Publications/MIConstitution.pdf
[4] "Constitution of the State of Washington," Washington State Legislature, accessed on May 21, 2024, available at https://leg.wa.gov/CodeReviser/pages/waconstitution.aspx

Whether we are entrepreneurs, parents, students, members of a trade group, or even a lawmaker, it is important to have meaningful public notice of when a bill is going to be available for a public hearing and what the actual text of that proposal is. Only then can we rearrange our schedules, review, and prepare to provide the testimony lawmakers need to help advance good policy for the state.

Requiring at least a three day notice of bills scheduled for a public hearing will help improve the information available not only for citizens but also lawmakers, as bills advance through the legislative process.

II. **Provide details of policies under consideration**

An engaged citizenry should be the pursuit not the torment of democracy. Adopting policies favoring government transparency at all levels of government is of utmost importance to the progression of free market ideals. Providing citizens with notice of public meetings and meaningful details of the topics on agendas is the first step towards more government transparency.

In a survey by CivicsPlus of 16,000 people, 82% wanted more government transparency at the local level.[5] The same survey also found that individuals engaging with city websites more than once a month were five times more trusting of their city council. As local governments share information, engage with constituents, and increase dialogue, more trust in government is built.

This trust is a time-saving effort. Government officials spend less time on dispersing information when a framework already exists. Also, an informed citizenry needs less time spent on history and background information and can move forward to solutions. These benefits of transparent government can be realized when:

---

[5] "CivicPlus Releases National Survey: The Link Between Technology, Government Transparency, and Resident Trust," CivicPlus, October 20, 2023, available at https://www.civicplus.com/news/nn/civicplus-releases-national-survey-results-showing-the-impact-of-technology-on-resident-trust-and-satisfaction-in-local-government/

1. **Public meetings are announced and available:** Public meetings should be announced on a regular platform, where it is easy for citizens to find and attend. Meetings should take advantage of the digital age and allow attendance through online meeting platforms – this includes remote testimony. Meetings should also be recorded for citizens to have access to and review previous material.

2. **Five days public notice of agenda:** It is difficult for citizens to come prepared to government meetings without knowing the agenda items before the meeting. Local government, including all councils, commissions, and boards should provide agenda items with at least five-day notice.

3. **Policy changes and proposals included in packet:** All policy changes and proposals included on a public meeting agenda for any level of government should have related documents and information publicly available before the meeting. If the item is included in the agenda and up for discussion, information should be included before the meeting explaining the issue. This includes the actual text of ordinances (etc.) to be considered.

Efforts towards more open public meetings are ongoing throughout the country. For example, the Transparent Idaho website has already taken a great step towards open and transparent government finances by providing spending information for the cities and school boards.[6] The Town Hall Idaho website also provides a list of all upcoming public meetings and links to virtual platforms when available.[7] The natural next step is for the documents and proposed measures under consideration to also be available when notice of a public meeting is made.

---

[6] "Transparent Idaho," accessed on May 21, 2024, available at https://localtransparency.idaho.gov/

[7] "Townhall Idaho," accessed on May 21, 2024, available at https://townhall.idaho.gov/

One of the few benefits of the pandemic was increased government transparency. All levels of government adopted virtual meetings and had electronic notice of meetings (at least to the board).[8] Pandemic angst and frustrations increased public participation in government meetings. Unfortunately, among state and local authorities, some entities are ending live streaming and remote participation. There is no good reason for this reduction in public access.

State and local governments should embrace increased transparency and provide access to the same details provided to public officials when issuing a public notice of a meeting and agenda. Citizens will benefit when government meetings are public for everyone (online and in-person), a five-day notice is provided, and relevant information is publicly included in the agenda notice before the meeting.

III. Authorize an open government ombudsman

To ensure public accountability and maintain control over the actions of government officials, state laws across the country authorize access to public records and require open public meetings. Though these rights exist on paper, they are not self-executing and often can result in costly litigation as the people attempt to enforce open government laws. One reform that could help serve as an advocate for the people's right to know would be the authorization of an official open government ombudsman.

This type of citizen-focused open government expert would help reduce the possibility of litigation when a public records dispute occurs. A similar concept is currently used in Connecticut. That state uses a Freedom of Information Commission to help mediate access to public records. Under Connecticut state law:[9]

---

[8] "Pandemic forced Idaho government agencies to livestream meetings. No reason to stop now," by Scott McIntosh, Idaho Stateman, September 22, 2022, available at https://www.idahostatesman.com/opinion/from-the-opinion-editor/article266041746.html

[9] "Connecticut Freedom of Information Commission," accessed on May 21, 2024, available at https://portal.ct.gov/foi/common-elements/template-v4/how-do-i_b#AppealCommission

"Any person denied the right to inspect or copy records under section 1-210 or wrongfully denied the right to attend any meeting of a public agency or denied any other right conferred by the Freedom of Information Act may appeal therefrom to the Freedom of Information Commission, by filing a notice of appeal with said commission."

Another example is New Jersey's Government Records Council:[10]

"The Government Records Council:

☐ Responds to inquiries and complaints about the law from the public and public agency records custodians

☐ Issues public information about the law and services provided by the Council

☐ Maintains a toll-free helpline and website to assist the public and records custodians

☐ Issues advisory opinions on the accessibility of government records

☐ Delivers training on the law

☐ Provides mediation of disputes about access to government records

☐ Resolves disputes regarding access to government records"

State constitutions generally start with a strong acknowledgment of the power of the people. For example, Idaho's constitution proclaims: "All political power is inherent

[10] "State of New Jersey Government Records Council," accessed on May 21, 2024, available at https://www.nj.gov/grc/about/

in the people." Idaho's Public Records Law Manual also clearly explains: "Open government is the cornerstone of a free society."[11]

The foundations for an accountable government can be found in strong citizen oversight, and one of the most critical tools to achieve this is open government laws. Authorizing an open government ombudsman would provide a helpful resource for citizens and potentially reduce the possibility of litigation relating to the enforcement of state public records and open meeting laws.

IV. Require legislative oversight of emergency powers

Though time is said to heal all wounds, the scars from the pandemic lockdowns remain fresh as the nation experienced executive overreach at the federal and state levels. It is important going forward for a proper check and balance to exist. The legislative branch must remain firmly in control of policy, even during times of an emergency.

There's no question that in a real emergency, governors need broad powers to act fast. Legislative bodies take time to assemble, so they can temporarily transfer their powers to the executive in an emergency.

But when problems do last for extended periods, it is the responsibility of legislators to debate risks, benefits, and trade-offs of various long-term approaches. Lawmakers may end up passing the very policies a governor would prefer, but they do it after deliberation as representatives of the people and do it in a public process.

It's the legislature, not the executive branch, that should make the laws we live under, and the executive – no matter the state or the person – is supposed to implement only laws passed by the legislature.

---

[11] "Idaho Public Records Law Manual," Idaho Attorney General, January 2023, available at
https://www.ag.idaho.gov/content/uploads/2018/04/PublicRecordsLaw.pdf

State examples of legislative oversight for emergency declarations

No emergency declaration should be indefinite or remain in place without legislative approval. There are many examples across the country of states ensuring this proper balance of power occurs.

In Wisconsin, for example, a state of emergency cannot exceed 60 days unless it is extended by the Legislature, and in Minnesota, a governor must call a special session if a "peace time" emergency lasts longer than 30 days.

To allow a governor to quickly respond to an emergency while still requiring appropriate legislative oversight, lawmakers could adopt this type of compromise for emergency powers:

> "No emergency order issued by the Governor may continue for longer than 30 days unless extended by the legislature through concurrent resolution. If the legislature is not in session, the emergency order may be extended in writing by the leadership of the senate and the house of representatives for 30 days or until the legislature can extend the emergency order by concurrent resolution. For purposes of this section, 'leadership of the senate and the house of representatives' means the majority and minority leaders of the senate and the speaker and the minority leader of the house of representatives. An emergency order narrowly written solely to qualify for federal funds is exempt from the requirement to receive legislative extension."

Policymaking should never be done by one person behind closed doors, even during an emergency. The number of days an emergency declaration remains in effect is less important than the requirement that the policies imposed be subject to legislative review and consent. Lawmakers must ensure that emergency powers statutes have this proper balance of power before the next emergency is declared.

V. Prohibit secret negotiations with public sector unions

Collective bargaining in government is controversial, but it should never be a secret.

Collective bargaining talks are the negotiations government unions have with government officials over salaries, benefits and working conditions. Because they involve millions of dollars of taxpayer money, they should be open and transparent. This doesn't mean the public participates in the negotiations, but the public should be allowed to observe the process.

This kind of process is not only good for taxpayers, but also for union members who are able to see how their union leadership is representing them at the bargaining table.

Idaho law prevents cities and unions from negotiation any contracts in secret. Democrats and Republicans passed the law unanimously and it was signed into law by former Governor Butch Otter in 2015.

Washington state, however, is a different story. While numerous attempts have been made to bring sunshine to the secretive process, government unions have resisted every step of the way.

The latest saga comes from Spokane, where unions sued the citizens who overwhelmingly approved a 2019 charter change that would have required sunlight on the process. The city didn't seem interested in the oversight, and because of its weak defense, the courts tossed the voter-approved change.

But various forms of open, transparent negotiations continue in more than half the states – including Idaho - and taxpayers and union members are better for it.

In Montana, Article II, Section 9 of the Montana State Constitution contains a sweeping government transparency requirement[12]:

> "No person shall be deprived of the right to examine documents or to observe the deliberations of all public bodies or agencies of state government and its subdivisions, except in cases in which the demand of individual privacy clearly exceeds the merits of public disclosure."

Ideally, contract negotiations should be fully open to the public. But at a minimum, government officials should adopt an openness process like the one used by the City of Costa Mesa, California, to keep the public informed. The city's policy is called Civic Openness in Negotiations, or COIN.

Under COIN, all contract proposals and documents to be discussed in closed- door negotiations are made publicly available before and after the meetings, with fiscal analysis showing the potential costs. While not full-fledged open meetings, access to all of the documents better informs the public about promises and tradeoffs being proposed with their tax dollars before an agreement is reached.

This openness also makes clear whether one side or the other is being unreason- able in its demands, and quickly reveals whether anyone is acting in bad faith. It's a hybrid solution that could be adopted by local officials if full open meetings are not allowed.[13]

VI. Consider open primaries without imposing controversial Ranked Choice Voting (RCV)

---

[12] Montana State Constitution, Article II, Section 9, available at https://leg.mt.gov/bills/mca/title_0000/article_0020/part_0010/section_0090/0000-0020-0010-0090.html

[13] Collective Bargaining Transparency, by Jason Mercier and F. Vincent Vernuccio, Better Cities.org, available at https://better-cities.org/wp-content/uploads/2020/11/BCP-collective-bargaining-transparency.pdf

There is a debate occurring in several states about whether to move from a closed primary to an open primary for elections. Unfortunately, this policy debate has sometimes also been intertwined with imposing Ranked Choice Voting (RCV).

Ranked choice voting continues to be controversial across the country.

In 2020, 50.55% of voters in Alaska adopted a Top Four and RCV ballot measure. The new process has been so unpopular, however, that Alaska voters will have the opportunity in 2024 to repeal it with the certification of a new ballot measure. Polling in Alaska has consistently shown that voters want to repeal ranked-choice voting.

Example of ranked-choice voting repeal in Washington

Washington State has had experience both with an open primary and with local voters in Pierce County adopting and then quickly repealing RCV.

Here are details on the state's voter approved Top Two open primary:[14]

> "The Top Two Primary was passed by the people in 2004 as an initiative. Initiative 872 passed by almost 60%. In 2005, before the new law was implemented, the Washington state Democratic, Republican, and Libertarian Parties sued in federal court. The lower courts imposed an injunction prohibiting the state from implementing the new Primary, but in March 2008, the U.S. Supreme Court upheld the new law. Washington state used the new Primary for the first time in the 2008 Primary and General Elections."

---

[14] "Top 2 Primary: FAQs for Voters," Washington Secretary of State, accessed on May 21, 2024, available at https://www.sos.wa.gov/elections/voters/helpful-information/top-2-primary-faqs-voters

As for RCV, this is from a 2009 blog post by the Washington Secretary of State's Office discussing why 71% of Pierce County voters repealed ranked-choice voting after using the system only once:[15]

VIDEO: Why ranked choice voting is bad public policy

> "It has always been kind of confusing to explain, but advocates believed it would be extremely popular and then possibly catch on elsewhere. Its biggest usage was last year when a new County Executive and other offices were filled this way, running in tandem with the regular state primary and general elections. It went downhill from there. Voters participating in an auditor's survey said by a 2-to-1 margin that they didn't like the system. And this year, it was back on the ballot – and voters have thrown it out by a 71-29 margin."

Washington's current Secretary of State Steve Hobbs remains opposed to ranked-choice voting:[16]

> "Ranked-choice voting adds a layer of complexity to voting that threatens to disenfranchise people who aren't experts at the process. This includes people living with developmental disabilities – such as my son – for whom choosing one candidate is more straightforward than figuring out how to rank a list of them. Additionally, it can be a challenge for newly naturalized citizens to adapt to American elections. Converting some elections to ranked-choice voting

---

[15] "Pierce Voters Nix 'Ranked-Choice Voting'," Washington Secretary of State, November 10, 2009, available at
https://blogs.sos.wa.gov/fromourcorner/index.php/2009/11/pierce-voters-nix-ranked-choice-voting/
[16] "Open Primaries and Ranked Choice Voting: A Conversation with WA's Secretary of State," by Jason Mercier, Mountain States Policy Center, September 15, 2023, available at
https://www.mountainstatespolicy.org/open-primaries-and-ranked-choice-voting-a-conversation-with-wa-s-secretary-of-state

would increase the obstacles to exercising their rights as Americans. Top-two primaries present none of these challenges. You pick your favorite, then you send in your ballot. That's something people can easily grasp. I stand firmly behind Top Two and encourage other states to learn from our usage of it."

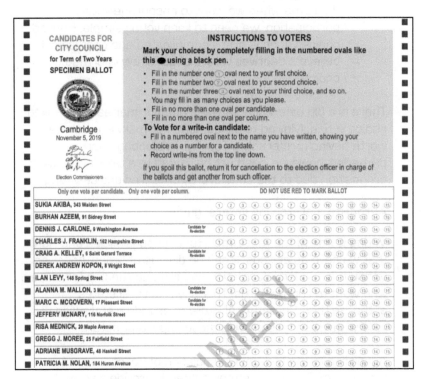

In 2024, Princeton University professor Nolan McCarty conducted a study of ranked-choice elections in New York City and Alaska and found that minority voters are disproportionately impacted by this type of election process. Professor McCarty noted:

> "In recent years, ranked-choice voting has been hyped as a solution to many perceived problems in American elections. Unfortunately, the hype has often outpaced the evidence. My research raises major concerns about whether RCV may work to further

reduce the electoral influence of racial and ethnic minority communities."[17]

Former California Governor Jerry Brown may have said it best when vetoing a RCV bill in 2016:

"In a time when we want to encourage voter participation, we need to keep voting simple. Ranked choice voting is overly complicated and confusing. I believe it deprives voters of genuinely informed choice."[18]

There is a big difference between open primaries and ranked-choice voting. Moving to a clean open primary is a debate worth having (preferably a Top Two). Adopting open primaries, however, need not be limited to a take-it-or-leave-it proposition tied to the controversy of ranked-choice voting.

VII.   Authorize a statewide voters' guide

Voting is one of the most important responsibilities and rights that we have as citizens. It can be difficult at times, however, to find the needed information about those running for office who want to represent us. This is why several states authorize their Secretary of State to provide a statewide voters' guide to help provide these important details.

According to the National Association of Secretaries of States (NASS), several states currently provide a voters' guide including Alabama, Alaska, California, Florida, Oregon, and Washington.

Here is how the Alaska Secretary of State explains this resource:

---

[17] "Ranked-Choice Voting Hurts Minorities: Study," Center for Election Confidence, January 11, 2024, available at https://electionconfidence.org/2024/01/11/ranked-choice-voting-hurts-minorities-study/
[18] "Brown vetoes bill to broaden ranked-choice voting in California," San Francisco Gate, September 30, 2016, available at https://www.sfgate.com/politics/article/Brown-vetoes-bill-to-broaden-ranked-choice-voting-9518031.php

"During a Primary and General election year the Division of Elections publishes two official pamphlets designed to help Alaskan voters make informed choices. Pamphlets are available in printed, digital, and audio formats; and made available to the public no later than 22 days prior to Election Day. Printed versions are mailed to every voter household and digital versions are posted to this page. Digital versions of the pamphlets are also available in select languages."

Along with a traditional printed and online voters' guide, another resource worth considering is a Video Voters' Guide. This would allow voters to go to one place to see and hear candidates in their own words about why they are running for office.

A voters' guide usually provides basic demographic and background information about candidates, generally in their own words, to help voters have a standardized reference for learning more about those seeking office. Providing a statewide voter guide is not only popular amongst voters, but it is also a best practice that all states should consider to help provide citizens access information they need to make informed decisions about those wishing to represent them.

VIII. Do not join the National Popular Vote compact

Seventeen states and the District of Columbia have joined in an agreement to award their Electoral College votes in a U.S. election to the winner of the national popular vote.

The National Popular Vote compact (NPV), as it is called, has gained steam over the past 25 years, lead mostly by liberal leaning states eager to work around the Electoral College.

The legislation, which is identical in each state, requires the state to award its electoral votes to the candidate who receives the most popular votes nationwide. This could mean a candidate that doesn't win a particular state could still receive the state's electoral votes.

States that have joined the National Popular Vote compact

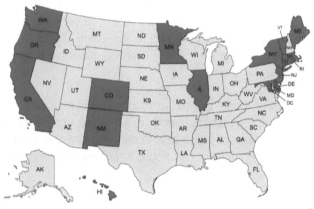

It is not unusual for a state to decide to allocate electoral votes differently. Two states, for example, allocate electoral votes based on the winner in each of the state's Congressional districts. Other states have a winner take all system.

But the NPV is problematic for several reasons. First, arguments about who won a close election would never end. Instead of being confined to one state or another based on the number of electoral votes a candidate may need, disputes would go national and parties could pick and choose areas to contest based on how many supporters the area may have.

Second, there are serious Constitutional questions, specifically regarding whether states can create a compact such as this without Congressional approval, and perhaps more importantly, whether the NPV violates the 14th Amendment, which says:

"No state shall make or enforce any law which shall abridge the privileges or immunities of citizens of the United States."

The NPV compact specifically nullifies a citizen's vote if the state's electoral votes are simply transferred to the winner of the national popular vote.

Analysts at the Cato Institute have noticed another trend now appearing in more conservative states to counteract any implementation of the NPV compact[19]:

"In North Dakota, the Republican-controlled state senate passed a bill saying their state will withhold its popular vote totals for president until after the Electoral College has voted in December. Instead, the state would only publish the rough percentages. This is deliberately aimed at making it impossible to properly calculate the national popular vote total in time to award electors on that basis. Similar bills have been introduced in other states."

As of 2024, Washington state has joined the NPV compact, but Idaho, Montana and Wyoming have not. To protect the legitimacy of elections and to preserve a voice in the Electoral College, they should avoid doing so.

---

[19] The fatally flawed national popular vote plan, by Andy Craig, Cato Institute, November 2021, available at https://www.cato.org/blog/fatally-flawed-national-popular-vote-plan

I.   More spending does not equal better results

K-12 public school spending is at an all-time high, and America spends more per student than any other developed nation.

Nationwide, the Education Data Initiative says we spend, on average, $16,390 per student, per year for K-12 public schools.[1]

The states that spend the most do not have the best outcomes. The states that spend the least do not have the worst outcomes.

State	Spending per student, per year	NAEP 4th Grade Reading Rank[2]	NAEP 4th Grade Math Rank[3]	NAEP 8th Grade Reading Rank[4]	NAEP 8th Grade Math Rank[5]	Graduation Rate[6]
Idaho	$8,748	30th	23rd	6th	3rd	80.1%
Washington	$19,523	23rd	27th	14th	18th	82.3%
Montana	$15,035	11th	15th	15th	14th	85.7%
Wyoming	$19,887	2nd	1st	16th	6th	81.8%
Utah	$9,479	7th	8th	3rd	2nd	88.2%
New York	$30,282	36th	46th	13th	23rd	87.0%
Illinois	$20,887	16th	18th	11th	20th	87.3%
Florida	$11,773	3rd	4th	21st	32nd	87.3%
Arizona	$9,072	28th	37th	30th	33rd	76.6%

---

[1] Education Data Initiative, September 2023, K-12 spending data, available at https://educationdata.org/public-education-spending-statistics

[2] 2022 – The Nation's Report Card, National Assessment of Education Progress Results, available at https://www.nationsreportcard.gov/profiles/stateprofile?sfj=NP&chort=2&sub=MAT&sj=&st=MN&year=2022R3

[3] Ibid

[4] Ibid

[5] Ibid

[6] U.S. News and World Report, state by state graduation rates for 2021-22 school year, available at https://www.usnews.com/education/best-high-schools/articles/see-high-school-graduation-rates-by-state

Since the 1970's, public school spending in the United States has surged. But much of the money is being spent outside the classroom.

A closer look at data since the turn of the century shows a dramatic increase in the number of administrative staff (88% higher) and principals and assistant principals (37% higher), than teachers and students (8% higher).

Growth in Administration, Principals, Teachers & Students in Public Schools
% Change Since 2000 – Digest of Education Statistics

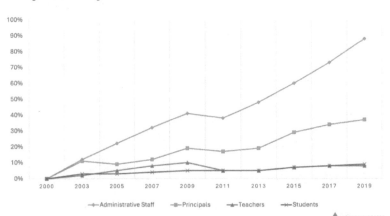

Despite the fact states have significantly increased K-12 funding, claims are still made that schools are underfunded, and more taxpayer resources are needed.

In both Idaho and Washington, more than 50% of the state budget is allocated to K-12. But while spending has gone up, student achievement has not. There is little correlation between increased education spending and achievement. If spending was the determining factor, the United States would have the best schools in the world, as the U.S. spends more than any other developed nation.

National Assessment of Education Progress

The Nation's Report Card – 8th Grade Math – 2002-2022

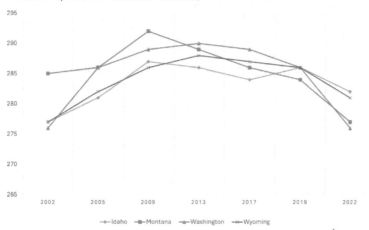

The Nation's Report Card – 8th Grade Reading – 2002-2022

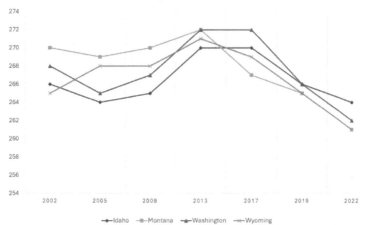

The Nation's Report Card - 4th Grade Reading - 2002-2022

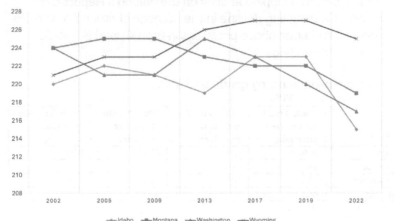

The Nation's Report Card - 4th Grade Math - 2002-2022

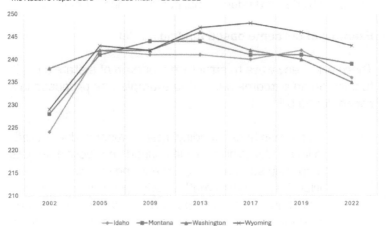

In addition to dropping scores on the Nation's Report Card, there is a troubling decline in the number of students who are considered at or above proficient in both 4th and 8th grade math and reading.

At or above proficient, by grade and state
The Nation's Report Card, 2022

State	Grade 4 math at or above proficient	Grade 4 reading at or above proficient	Grade 8 math at or above proficient	Grade 8 reading at or above proficient
Idaho	36%	32%	32%	32%
Montana	38%	34%	29%	29%
Washington	35%	34%	32%	28%
Wyoming	44%	38%	30%	31%

II.   Focus education funding on outcomes

To refocus this debate, efforts should be made to tie new spending to desired educational performance outcomes.

Example of outcome-based funding model

There are many ways to structure a portion of a state's K-12 funding on an outcome basis. One example was proposed in a recent Idaho bill:

> "Outcomes-based funding' means funding distributed to local education agencies based on meeting targets in specific student achievement and learning priorities, including mathematics proficiency and growth in grades 5 through 8, and attainment of the credentials necessary for transition into workforce or postsecondary education in grades 9 through 12. This funding shall be aligned with the strategic student achievement goals determined by the legislature and the state board of education and measured and tracked by the state department of education and division of career technical education."[7]

---

[7] "HB 557 – 2024," Idaho Legislature, available at
https://legislature.idaho.gov/sessioninfo/2024/legislation/H0557/

It's no longer good enough to simply say all problems would be solved if only the system had more money. In the end, outcomes-based funding encourages districts to focus on student performance, and not just enrollment. In the effort to improve student outcomes, it is a policy worth pursuing.

III.   **Put the principal in charge of the school**

Research shows that one of the most effective tools for improving school outcomes is to put the principal in charge of the school. What exactly does this mean? Isn't the principal already in charge of the school? Not exactly.

In many districts, principals are simply the manager rather than the leader. Principals should, instead, be considered the CEOs of their schools. They should be given a budget, and then decide how to spend it. They should have the authority to hire and fire their staff. They should have the authority to shape educational programs that best suit their students' needs. And after all of this happens, they should be held responsible for student outcomes.

This kind of education reform is not complicated, and had been successfully adopted in places like Baltimore, where former CEO Dr. Andres Alonso put his faith in his principals.[8] School principals became responsible for more than 80% of their budgets, and those who were unsuccessful were removed.[9]

> "Many principals were excited regarding the new changes and greater levels of responsibility, now having control of the school budget, curriculum and staffing decisions and developing strategies for school improvement. Dr. Alonso and the team understood

---

[8] Former Baltimore schools CEO Andres Alonso said to be a candidate for Newark school superintendent role, ChalkBeat, April 2018, available at https://www.chalkbeat.org/newark/2018/4/27/21104967/former-baltimore-schools-ceo-andres-alonso-said-to-be-a-candidate-for-newark-school-superintendent-r/
[9] Driving change in Baltimore City Public Schools, An Interview with Andres Alonso, District Management Group, available at https://dmj.dmgroupk12.com/articles/driving-change-in-baltimore-city-public-schools-an-interview-with-andr-s-alonso

that no two schools are necessarily alike and each has a unique context with specific needs. Now, principals had to think much differently about their work. For example, in the past there were examples of principals who felt there was little that could be done regarding curriculum materials that did not meet the reading needs of upper grade students. With the change, principals and teachers had much greater authority and investment in and responsibility for making decisions that best meet the particular learning needs for students at the school level. And as a result, principals were being held accountable for doing so."[10]

The results were astounding. Not only did student outcomes improve, but schools were removed from federal "needs to improve" lists.[11] Unfortunately, as Baltimore has moved away from this approach, student results have suffered.

IV.   **Provide students and families with Education Savings Accounts or education choice tax credits**

No education policy is a panacea for perfect outcomes. Every system and every school will produce failures, and there will always be opportunities for improvement and lessons learned. "Education choice" simply means allowing some state funding to follow the student to the education method or school of their choice, rather than allotting all funds to the public school district where the student resides. Education choice means an all of the above approach – traditional public schools, charter schools, magnet schools, micro-schools, homeschooling, and more.

[10] The case of Dr. Andres Alonso: Principles of leadership, by Jared R. Lancer, Ed.D., August 20, 2021, available at https://www.linkedin.com/pulse/case-dr-andres-alonso-principles-leadership-practice-r-lancer-ed-d-/
[11] Baltimore City Public Schools: Implementing Bounded Autonomy, Harvard Graduate School of Education, April 6, 2011, available at https://projects.iq.harvard.edu/files/pelp/files/pel063p21.pdf

Education choice policies such as Education Savings Accounts (ESAs) or education choice tax credits shift decision-making power to those closest to the student (parents) who are best able to assess that student's unique education needs. While some families can afford to opt out of the state-sponsored system, the majority cannot.

VIDEO: What is education choice and how can it improve outcomes?

The competition and innovation generated by education choice require schools to be more responsive to student needs, allowing great schools to flourish and forcing poor schools to improve. A family is never worse off by having more than one education choice.

There are 187 studies on the impact of education choice – and the results are overwhelming

Every state is different. Every child is different. It shouldn't matter what school a child is attending, so long as they are receiving a quality education. Based on the strong results from nearly 190 studies, it's easy to understand why increasing numbers of Americans support education choice. The facts and the research don't lie.

As of March 2023, there have been nearly 190 studies on the impact of education choice. Researchers have looked at empirical data showing the fiscal effects, parental satisfaction, test scores, attainment, civic values, school safety, and racial integration.

Remarkably, 84% of studies show a positive effect, 10% show no impact, and 6% show a negative result.

Studies on impact of education choice options
As of 2024

Outcome	Number of Studies	Positive Effect	No Effect	Negative Effect
Program Participant Test Scores	17	61%	22%	17%
Educational Attainment	7	71%	29%	0%
Parent Satisfaction	33	91%	3%	6%
Public School Student Test Scores	29	90%	3%	7%
Civic Values and Practices	11	55%	45%	0%
Integration	8	88%	13%	0%
Fiscal Effects	74	87%	6%	6%
School Safety	8	100%	0%	0%
Total	187	84%	10%	6%

Fact-checking claims made against additional education choice options

Several false claims are routinely made against education choice options such as ESA's or education tax credits. Here are the most common:

- *False claim: "This is a voucher scheme."* By the very definition, tax credits or ESAs are not vouchers. Tax credits are the simplest form of education choice. In the end, tax credits are given to parents directly and vouchers are given to schools or a specific institution.

- *False Claim: "This defunds neighborhood schools."* Tax credits take zero funds out of a state's public school budget. They are a separate line item just like other policy proposals. Comparatively speaking, tax credits are generally a small fraction of a state's overall K-12 public school allocation.

- *False claim: "This will only help the wealthy."* Wealthy parents currently have the privilege of making two types of educational choices. They can either opt to reside in areas with reputable public schools or they can afford to enroll their children in private schools by paying the necessary fees. Consequently, educational choice initiatives are typically tailored to cater to the requirements of disadvantaged students and those from low-income backgrounds.

Median household income of those participating in Arizona & Indiana education choice programs

Data provided by the Indiana and Arizona Departments of Education

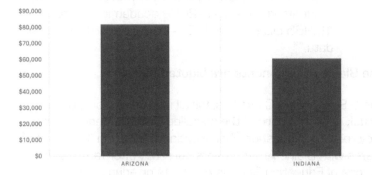

By erecting barriers that prevent low-income families from accessing the highest quality education, we are essentially impeding the advancement of disadvantaged children, which is both unfair and unnecessary.

☐ *False claim: "These programs haven't helped students in other states."* As previously mentioned, there have been nearly 190 empirical studies on the impact of education choice. Researchers have looked at fiscal effects, parent satisfaction, test scores, attainment, civic values, school safety, and racial integration. Remarkably, 84% of studies show a positive effect, 10% show no impact, and 6% show a negative result.

☐ *False claim: "Rural communities will be hurt."* It cannot be said that education choice will not help in rural areas because there are few or no alternatives, and then, at the same time, that education choice will destroy the district school system because so many students will leave for alternative options. Since

Florida enacted its tax-credit scholarship policy 20 years ago "the number of private schools in Florida's 30 rural counties has grown from 69 to 120" and "private school enrollment in those counties has more than doubled, from 5,354 rural private school students in the 2001–2002 academic year to 10,965 students in 2021–2022, according to state data."[12]

The Blaine Amendments are bigoted relics

The U.S. Supreme Court has, for all intents and purposes, struck down the core of the so-called Blaine Amendments as they relate to education choice options. As a result, dozens of states with Blaine Amendments currently offer families the options of Education Savings Accounts or education choice tax credits.

Like many other states (more than two-thirds, to be exact), Idaho adopted its Blaine Amendment at the time of statehood in 1890. The language, which was debated as a federal constitutional amendment as well, essentially prohibits the use of state funds for any religious purposes. Article IX, Section 5 of the Idaho State Constitution reads:

> "Neither the legislature nor any county, city, town, township, school district, or other public corporation, shall ever make any appropriation, or pay from any public fund or moneys whatever, anything in aid of any church or sectarian or religious society, or for any sectarian or religious purpose, or to help support or sustain any school, academy, seminary, college, university or other literary or scientific institution, controlled by any church, sectarian or religious denomination whatsoever..."

Why was this such an issue in the country at the time of adoption in the 19th century? Put simply, it was fear of

---

[12] "Rustic Renaissance: Education Choice in Rural America," Heritage Foundation, January 9, 2023, available at https://www.heritage.org/sites/default/files/2023-01/SR264_0.pdf

Catholics. As the Catholic population grew, bigotry aimed to keep public funds in schools that were teaching - even praying - under a Protestant umbrella.

More than 130 years later, opponents of additional education options for children have used the outdated relic of the Blaine Amendments as an excuse to block any legislation that might expand education options for families.
Two recent U.S. Supreme Court cases have curtailed Blaine Amendment restrictions: *Espinoza v. Montana Department of Revenue* (2020) and *Carson v. Makin* (2022).

The *Espinoza* decision held that government attempts to exclude religious schools from public scholarship or tax credits are subject to strict scrutiny, meaning lawmakers must prove they have a "compelling interest" in restricting the free exercise of religion of scholarship or tax credit recipients.[13] The *Carson* majority held that "a neutral benefit program in which public funds flow to religious organizations through the independent choices of private benefit recipients does not offend the Establishment Clause."[14]

In other words, states cannot fall back on their Blaine Amendments to justify prohibitions on public funding of schools solely due to their religion. In addition, a state cannot discriminate against religious beneficiaries of public scholarships or tax credits by forbidding them from using those benefits at religious schools. As the Institute for Justice writes, "these obstacles to education freedom are now largely a dead letter."[15]

The allocation of public funds in this context is determined by the private choices of individuals, rather than any direct governmental action to funnel public resources into religious or private educational institutions. The courts have

---

[13] Epinoza v. Montana Department of Revenue, Supreme Court of the United States, 2019, available at https://www.supremecourt.gov/opinions/19pdf/18-1195_g314.pdf
[14] Carson v. Makin, Supreme Court of the United States, 2022, available at https://www.supremecourt.gov/opinions/21pdf/20-1088_dbfi.pdf
[15] The Blaine Amendments, Insitute for Justice, available at https://ij.org/issues/school-choice/blaine-amendments/

underscored that this mechanism does not result in the state endorsing or establishing any religion.

More than half the country provides ESAs or education choice tax credits/scholarships

As of the Spring of 2024, the number of states providing parents and students with the option for Education Savings Accounts, education choice tax credits, or an education tax scholarship reached 29.[16] Several states are also in the process of expanding their existing education choice programs to cover even more students. Here is the Spring 2024 map of the 29 states with these education choice options.

States with ESAs, education choice tax credits or education tax scholarships

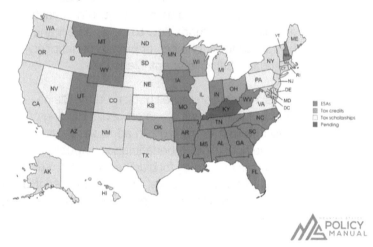

☐ 18 states with ESAs: Utah, Montana, Wyoming, Arizona, Iowa, Missouri, Arkansas, Louisiana, Tennessee, Mississippi, Indiana, Alabama, Georgia, Florida, South Carolina, North Carolina, West Virginia, and New Hampshire.

---

[16] "School Choice In America," Ed Choice, accessed on May 22, 2024, available at https://www.edchoice.org/school-choice-in-america-dashboard-scia/

- 4 states with education choice tax credits: Oklahoma, Minnesota, Wisconsin, and Ohio.

- 7 states with education tax scholarships: Nevada, South Dakota, Nebraska, Kansas, Virginia, Pennsylvania, and Rhode Island.

- 1 state pending: Kentucky (education choice constitutional amendment passed legislature; pending voter approval).

Idaho, Washington, Oregon, and California are now the only states in the West not providing either an ESA, education choice tax credit, or education tax scholarship option for families. In fact, the Heritage Foundation's education report card gave Idaho[17] a ranking of 29th and Washington[18] a ranking of 43rd when it came to education choice.

Lawmakers in Idaho and Washington should consider the education reforms advancing in the rest of the country and provide students and families with more options.

V.   Adopt the Public School Transparency Act

School district budget documents are a maze of numbers and legal jargon – if you can even find them. Depending on the district, they can be buried on websites, and only accessible if you know where to look.

For example, Idaho's largest school district, the West Ada School District, has a budget that can be found online, but it is more than 300 pages long and includes six different funds and 36 different programs. In Montana, the Billings Public School district is the state's largest. Finding its budget on the

---

[17] Heritage Foundation education freedom report card, Idaho, 2022-23, available at
https://www.heritage.org/educationreportcard/pages/states/id.html
[18]Heritage Foundation education freedom report card, 2022-23, available at
https://www.heritage.org/educationreportcard/pages/states/wa.html#:~:text=Washingto
n%20remains%20ranked%20%2343%20in,and%20teacher%20freedom%20(%2349)

district's website is nearly impossible. Unfortunately, transparency doesn't mean much if it's not understandable.

The Public School Transparency Act

The Idaho Poll - Mountain States Policy Center - November 2022

The PSTA would require school districts to clearly show in their annual budget the total amount spent, the amount spent on each student, the percentage of spending going to the classroom, the average administrator and teacher compensation, and the latest student academic outcomes. Hearing this, would you support or oppose this law?

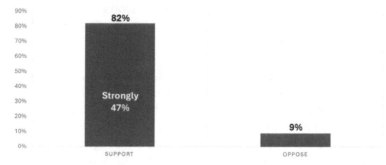

federal) spent by the district that year

2. *Amount of total dollars spent per student, per year*

3. *Amount and percentage of total dollars allocated to average classroom*

4. *Average administrator salary and benefits*

5. *Average teacher salary and benefits*

6. *Ratio of administrators to teachers to students*

Very little extra work would be needed to provide this data and make it accessible on paper and online. Most districts already have it buried somewhere in their budget documents. They know where to look, whereas parents and taxpayers can get lost. In the interest of transparency, school districts should be eager to share this information with the public.

Parents and taxpayers may see this data and conclude their school districts need more resources. Others may see it and believe that not enough is being done to spend money in the classroom. Regardless, the community will have a broader sense of the results being achieved, and what – if any – changes need to be made. A 2022 Idaho Poll showed more than 80% of citizens support this transparency concept.[19]

Idaho's top education official has also endorsed the idea:

> "It's a positive for our schools if the communities they serve understand how tax dollars are being spent," said Superintendent Debbie Critchfield said. "Let's face it, school budgets tend to be complex and [the Public School Transparency Act] is a step that helps simplify the way they're communicated publicly."

VIDEO: The Public School Transparency Act

Transparency can help improve student outcomes. After years of school shutdowns, controversial curriculum, and questions about resources, one thing is certain – the public needs more information to improve education.

VI. Increase the availability of public charter schools

Charter schools are tuition-free schools that are publicly funded but independently run. Most charter schools are exempt from many state laws and regulations but are subject to a contract that includes goals, fiscal oversight, and accountability. If charter schools don't perform, they can be closed. However, charter school laws vary from state to state. While Washington, for example, allows public charter schools, the law is so limiting that it produces an artificial cap on the number of students who can attend.

---

[19] "The results of MSPC's 2022 Idaho Poll," Mountain States Policy Center, December 14, 2022, available at https://www.mountainstatespolicy.org/the-results-of-mspc-s-2022-idaho-poll

Despite the claims of opponents, charter schools are public schools. They don't pick and choose students, and often they serve more underserved students than local district schools and achieve higher outcomes than traditional public schools.

Charter schools are showing positive performance outcomes for students

Public charter schools are making a positive difference in students' lives. That's the main conclusion from Stanford's Center for Research on Educational Outcomes (CREDO) 2023 analysis.[20] The CREDO study has been produced three times – once in 2009, again in 2013 and the latest version in 2023. More than 3.7 million students across 43 states attend charter schools, including in Idaho and Washington. Montana recently legalized public charter schools.

The latest CREDO report shows increases in outcomes for just about every student category in nearly all states. The typical charter school student had math and reading gains that outpaced peers in traditional public schools. In math, charter schools advanced learning by an additional six days. In reading, charter school students advanced 16 days of learning each year.

While these numbers are national averages, certain state-by-state data shows even stronger gains. Idaho's charter school students gained an additional 17 days of learning in reading. Washington's advancement approached 30 days. In Math, Washington students advanced almost 40 days while Idaho students advanced eight.

---

[20] "As A Matter Of Fact: The National Charter School Study III," Credo, accessed on May 22, 2024, available at https://ncss3.stanford.edu/

Average Annual Growth from Charter School Attendance
Reading & Math – CREDO Report, Stanford University

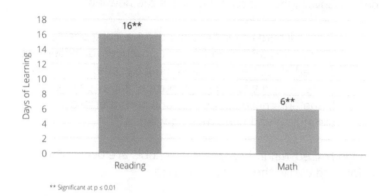

** Significant at p ≤ 0.01

POLICY MANUAL

Charter schools in Idaho continue to have an impressive record. There are more than 70 statewide, and some are listed as among the top schools in the nation.[21]

Charter schools and students, by state

State	Charter Schools	Charter Students
Idaho	72	28,051
Wyoming	5	642
Washington	17	4,571
Montana* (legal as of 2024)	0	0
Utah	137	77,733
Oregon	131	42,668
Nevada	94	63,944
California	1,324	678,830
Arizona	585	231,195
New Mexico	99	30,160
Colorado	273	130,279
Alaska	31	7,621

In 2024, Idaho adopted "The Accelerating Public Charter Schools Act" to remove some of the regulatory burden on

---

[21] "Best Idaho High Schools," US News, accessed on May 22, 2024, available at https://www.usnews.com/education/best-high-schools/idaho/rankings

charter schools to allow administrators and educators more time to focus on student outcomes. A press release by Idaho's Governor Little said this about the new law:

> "This bill cuts red tape around supporting charter schools in Idaho through best practices, development, and educational and operational assistance. It gives more flexibility for the high performing charters of Idaho and more support to charters that are struggling and need more guidance." [22]

Though limited in number, charter schools are also performing well in the Evergreen State.

> "Washington's charter school students are scoring similar or better than their traditional public school peers, according to a new report released by the State Board of Education. The report, which analyzes data from the 2022-2023 school year, also found Black and Hispanic students, English learners and children from low-income households are consistently performing better in charter schools than in traditional public schools." [23]

Policymakers in all states should continue to embrace charter schools and act to enhance their ability to meet the needs of students and families who are looking for alternative education opportunities.

VII. Adopt the College Career Transparency Act

High school students considering whether it is worth it to pursue a college degree usually consider two major questions: how much debt will I incur, and how much will I make when I finally achieve graduation and a career?

---

[22] "Idaho sets a strong example by enhancing charter schools," Mountain States Policy Center, March 2, 2024, available at https://www.mountainstatespolicy.org/idaho-sets-a-strong-example-by-enhancing-charter-schools

[23] "WA charter school performance on par with other public schools, state report says," Washington State Standard, April 22, 2024, available at https://washingtonstatestandard.com/2024/04/22/wa-charter-school-performance-on-par-with-other-public-schools-state-report-says/

Unfortunately, it can be very difficult to easily find the answers, which can result in students taking out large college loans for careers that might not provide the adequate salary to pay down the loans.

Between 1963 and 2021, the cost of attendance at a four-year college rose 165%. Increases can be found in both public institutions, where the average cost is now $19,374, and private, where students can now pay $45,920.[24] Interestingly, private, for-profit colleges have been successful in *lowering* their costs, from a peak of $31,709 in 2004, to $27,470 today.

It is not a given that the cost of college must increase. Consider the example being set by Purdue University. Purdue University has kept its tuition frozen for 13 years – at less than $10,000 per year.[25] Former Indiana Governor Mitch Daniels – who became President of Purdue – says it has been a top priority to keep the number affordable for families. As a result, student loan borrowing at Purdue has decreased by 40% since 2012. Now, 11 graduating classes at Purdue have never experienced a tuition increase.

Daniels says the key has been an effort to manage expenses and asking alumni for more contributions. But as Purdue has kept tuition frozen, student enrollment has increased, allowing the university to more easily balance its books.

While other higher education officials should learn from the Purdue example by adopting policies that make tuition more affordable, policymakers can also help provide data that informs a student's decision on which colleges to attend and degrees to pursue.

---

[24] "Digest of Education Statistics," National Center for Education Statistics, accessed on May 22, 2024, available at
https://nces.ed.gov/programs/digest/d21/tables/dt21_330.10.asp
[25] "Purdue trustees endorse 13th consecutive tuition freeze; approve updated housing, dining plans," Purdue University, December 8, 2023, available at
https://www.purdue.edu/newsroom/releases/2023/Q4/purdue-trustees-endorse-13th-consecutive-tuition-freeze-approve-updated-housing-dining-plans.html#:~:text=Tuition%20freeze%202025%2D26,state%20students%20through%202025%2D26.

Indiana resident annual tuition and fees

Purdue University

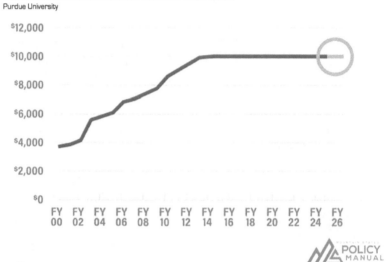

Increasing college costs and career outcome transparency

One option to make the decision easier is a concept called the Career Transparency Act or CTA. The CTA would require the state to make a variety of statistics and information publicly available to high school students considering a college path. The information would include:

☐ A listing of the state's future workforce needs;

☐ Starting wage information and education requirements for the top 25 high-demand jobs in the state;

☐ A listing of the 40 baccalaureate degree programs with the highest average annual wages following graduation;

☐ A listing of the 20 associate degree programs with the highest average annual wages following

74

graduation;

- [ ] The cost of obtaining the degree or certificate at state institutions of higher education, including;

  - o Tuition and fees
  - o Room and board
  - o Books and supplies
  - o Transportation
  - o Other costs

- [ ] The median wage earned by students who graduated with the certificate or degree;

- [ ] The median student debt of those who graduated with the certificate or degree;

- [ ] Progress on repaying student loans by those who graduated with the certificate or degree; and

- [ ] The percentage of students who withdraw from the institution and do not enroll in the program at another higher education institution.

With this information readily available, students could better understand whether the long-term career benefit would be worth such a large financial burden.

Policymakers may not be able to control all college costs, but they can help inform better career and financial decisions by students considering higher education. Identifying workforce needs, a listing of wages, clear information about the cost of obtaining a degree, and more should all be made readily available via the Career Transparency Act.

I. **Pillars of regulatory reform and oversight**

Regulations play a role in our everyday lives. Some dictate where and how we can eat. Others place restrictions on what we can sell or how we can operate a business.

For example, in Tamarack, Idaho, it was once illegal to buy onions after dark without a permit. Nationally, 18 U.S. Code 2074 makes it a crime to "knowingly issue or publish any counterfeit weather forecast." Bacon processing plants in California still require a fax machine.

Whether they be at the local, state, or federal level, all laws and regulations have a cost. In fact, a study by the Journal of Economic Growth concluded that regulations have slowed economic growth by as much as two percent per year.

Economically significant final rules by year
Office of the Federal Register

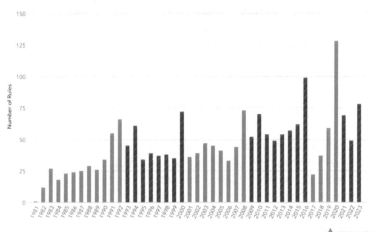

Economists at the Mercatus Center at George Mason University found the size of the regulation state significantly slows economic growth and has translated into a $13,000 loss in real income for every American.

Rules and regulations come in all shapes and sizes. They can be tallied by pages, words, and even economic significance. Luckily, policymakers in the Mountain States have recognized the need to limit the regulatory burden. Idaho Governor Brad Little has touted his Red Tape Reduction Act – an effort to make Idaho one of the least regulated states in the nation. Numerous national reports give Idaho top marks for the effort.

Montana Governor Greg Gianforte has labeled red tape reduction as one of his top priorities. In the most recent Montana legislative session, he signed into law more than 100 bills to eliminate commissions, streamline applications, and do away with burdensome and outdated requirements.

These efforts should not be confused with an attempt to do away with every law, rule, and regulation. On the contrary, those that are well-designed and consistently reviewed protect not only business owners and workers but also consumers and citizens.

Still, lawmakers in the region and across the nation can and should do more. Thousands of rules and regulations no longer relevant or needed remain on the books.

The keys to regulatory reform

As policymakers consider the rules that govern rules and regulations, they should take care to ensure they are simple, predictable, and reviewable.

Number of final rules in Federal Register affecting small business

Office of the Federal Register – Significant rules at bottom of each bar

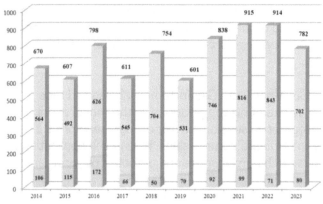

The fight to reduce ineffective and burdensome regulations has received the most traction at the state level. In 2023 alone, Idaho legislators have reviewed more than 120 new or updated rules from state bureaucracy, on topics including daycare licensing, bail agents, insurance fees, corporate governance, juvenile detention centers, podiatry, physical therapy, invasive species stickers, and more.

Idaho started on the path to its low regulatory burden with Governor Brad Little's Red Tape Reduction Act. It continued its effort with zero-based regulation – an executive order that forces regular reviews of rules and restrictions. In fact, roughly 20% of each of Idaho's agency rules are reviewed annually.

At the state level, policymakers should be doing more to reduce burdensome regulations and take responsibility for those still on the books. Perhaps the best way to accomplish this goal is to be committed to the separation of powers. In too many cases, bureaucrats take on the role of rulemaking and implementation – even though they were never elected to write laws. Legislatures should never delegate sweeping lawmaking authority to regulatory agencies.

Bureaucratic rules and regulations by state (as of 2022)

State	Rank (lowest)	Rules	Words
Idaho	1st	36,612	3,978,329
Montana	5th	59,902	4,761,522
Wyoming	8th	72,218	4,092,624
Washington	42nd	200,364	18,009,548
Oregon	43rd	209,207	19,057,361
California	50th	403,774	22,005,369

Executives have the responsibility of signing and implementing laws, and any rule that has the force of law should be signed by the Governor. Far too often, state rules are signed and put into place by unelected bureaucrats who may not need to consider the best interests or concerns of citizens because citizens cannot remove them from office. It is more difficult for a state's chief executive to claim he or she didn't know about a controversial rule if they were required to approve the rule before it took effect.

Judges are constitutionally required to interpret the law without bias. Unfortunately, many judges have decided to defer their role and responsibilities to agency interpretation. To ensure the judiciary understands and doesn't skirt its duty, judges should interpret statutes, regulations, and other documents without giving any deference to an agency's legal interpretation. If the text is still unclear, judges should default to a reasonable interpretation that limits agency power and maximizes individual liberty. In other words, the tie should go to the citizen, not the government.

Thanks to the separation of powers, ensuring oversight and lessening the regulatory burden are achievable. Each of the three branches has a role and responsibility. As the National Governors Association writes, "well designed regulations protect workers, consumers and the environment while promoting entrepreneurship and economic growth."

Idaho and Montana deserve credit for attempting to reform the regulatory state. But as new policymakers consider the rules that govern rules and regulations, they should take care to ensure they are always simple, predictable, and reviewable. Policymaking is the exclusive prerogative of the legislative branch of our government and should never be delegated to an unelected administrative body.

II. Adopt sunset provisions

One of the best ways to ensure laws and regulations do not become overly burdensome is to include sunset clauses or provisions. A sunset clause is an expiration date – requiring further legislative action if the legislation or regulation is to continue. This can be particularly helpful in a situation where a law was passed to address an urgent, timely situation, but no longer applies.

Unfortunately, tens of thousands of laws that were passed in the 19th and 20th century may be outdated, but they remain on the books, and therefore create a larger regulatory burden each year. Adding sunset clauses requires lawmakers to review the effectiveness and need of regulations and programs. Researchers at the Mercatus Center at George Mason University found a sunset review process can also be effective in minimizing the executive branch's influence on state boards and agencies.[1]

III. Embrace occupational licensing reform

State-specific, non-universal occupational licensing exists in 22% of professions and has grown over the last few decades, from 5% in the 1950s.[2] Why? It has nothing to do with the quality of service or requests from consumers. In many situations these are industry-created artificial barriers to entry, limiting competition in the market. Occupational licensing does the reverse of its promises: decreasing the

---

[1] Sunset Legislation in the States: Balancing the Legislature and the Executive, by Brian Baugus and Feler Bose, Mercatus Center, George Mason Unversity, August 2015, available at https://www.mercatus.org/research/research-papers/sunset-legislation-states-balancing-legislature-and-executive

[2] "Occupational Licensing," CATO, December 15, 2022, available at https://www.cato.org/publications/facilitating-personal-improvement-occupational-licensing

quality of service, increasing prices, decreasing employment, and frequently having a disproportionate effect on low to middle-income earners.

Share of occupations requiring a license in 2021
U.S. Bureau of Labor Statistics

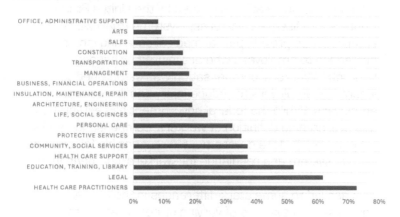

A frequent example of occupational licensing harm can be found among hair braiders. Many states have required hair braiders to attend cosmetology school. Except, with the glaring oversight that cosmetology school doesn't teach the braiding profession. Thankfully, many of the braiding licensing requirements have been overturned in recent years but while they existed, they caused unnecessary economic harm to many families.

Occupational licensing reform doesn't argue for poor service from any profession but recognizes that consumers encourage better quality through reviews and choice than the quality licensure creates. Many professions are better served by utilizing voluntary programs, removing unneeded licenses, and relying on service review websites like Yelp and Angie. Even the American Veterinary Medical Association has recognized the hassles and costs of state-specific licensure and is looking for better practices.

A life-changing event, like moving or employment changes, doesn't change abilities. It's time states recognize this conclusion and support occupational licensing reforms.

IV.   Use competition to reduce workers' compensation costs

Workers' compensation is defined by the United States Centers for Disease Control as, "systems [that] were established to provide partial medical care and income protection to employees who are injured or become ill from their job." Workers' compensation was established to incentivize employers to reduce injury and illness to their employees. While the federal government has established this overarching definition of workers' compensation and its purpose, each state government is responsible for creating its own system and regulation for workers' compensation.

This has led to some stark differences in the workers' compensation systems of varying states. Washington and Wyoming, for example, are two of just four states (North Dakota and Ohio are the others) with a monopoly worker's comp system. This top-down control without any competition has led to increasing rates and questionable customer service. Meanwhile, in Idaho and Montana, employers can choose to purchase their worker's compensation from the state, from private companies, or can self-insure, leading to declining rates.

While there is some debate about which system – private or state-controlled – works best, there is ample research to suggest the private model uses the free market to improve coverage, lower costs and protect workers.

Shifting to private competition

As we compare the public and private provisions of workers' compensation, we should consider the results of states that have shifted from entirely public to private systems.

West Virginia is an excellent example of this. In 2004, then-governor Joe Manchin and the Legislature approved legislation that privatized workers' compensation. In the years since workers' compensation rates for businesses have steadily declined thanks to the competition offered by dozens of private insurance companies. Prior to 2004 when the state oversaw workers' compensation in West Virginia, the system was losing $1 million dollars per day and had an unfunded $3 billion in liability. There were also loopholes that allowed individuals to take advantage of the system at taxpayers' expense - one could be declared permanently disabled at one job and collect lifetime benefits all while working at a new job.

However, since privatization in 2004, scams such as this have halted, as private companies compete to offer injured workers the best and timeliest coverage to get them back to work as soon as possible. This has provided major savings for both employers and taxpayers, and the consistent decline in rates since 2004 is proof that free markets and the competition they provide are essential.

West Virginia isn't the only state to switch from public to private workers' compensation systems. In 2000, Nevada also made the switch to workers' compensation provided by private companies and self-insurance. As with West Virginia, privatization had immediate positive effects on Nevada employers and taxpayers. In the 90s, the state's workers' compensation system was at risk of being insolvent due to a large deficit, and the state's fund had a projected unfunded liability of $3 billion. However, in the years since privatization, Nevada's workers' compensation rates have declined steadily.

Worker's compensation is important for employees and their employers. While nearly all states require businesses to purchase some form of workers' compensation to protect their employees and themselves, each state takes a different approach and presents a unique set of requirements. Policymakers should allow private options for workers' compensation - a free market solution that will promote competition and benefit businesses and employees alike.

V. Avoid costly minimum wage increases

Raising the minimum wage is a policy discussion ripe with tradeoffs. On the one hand, a hike in hourly pay could help some low income workers. On the other, small business owners would be hurt and, as a result, would likely employ fewer workers. The tradeoff is highlighted in the Mountain States.

Washington state, for example, has hiked its minimum wage to $16.28 per hour. Wyoming and Idaho have kept the minimum wage at the federal minimum of $7.25, while Montana's minimum wage sits at $10.30. Data from the Bureau of Labor Statistics shows Washington's unemployment rate is 71% higher than Wyoming's, 55% higher than Montana's and 45% higher than Idaho's.

State Minimum Wages & Unemployment Rates
Bureau of Labor Statistics

Economists across the political spectrum agree there are tradeoffs. The Congressional Budget Office (CBO) says[3]:

---

[3] How increasing the federal minimum wage could affect employment and family income, Congressional Budget Office, available at https://www.cbo.gov/publication/55681

> "In general, increasing the federal minimum wage would raise the earnings and family income of most low-wage workers and thus lift some families out of poverty—but doing so would cause other low-wage workers to become jobless, and their family income would fall."

The CBO's online tool allows users to plug in a minimum wage target and experience the consequences. For example, if the minimum wage were increased to $12 per hour, CBO data shows a decline in average weekly U.S. employment, as well as a drop in real family income.

Research from the Harvard Business Review had similar findings. It concluded:

> "For every $1 increase in the minimum wage, we found that the total number of workers scheduled to work each week increased by 27.7%, while the average number of hours each worker worked per week decrease by 20.8%. For an average store in California, these changes translated into four extra workers per week and five fewer hours per worker per week — which meant that the total wage compensation of an average minimum wage worker in a California store actually fell by 13.6%. This decrease in the average number of hours worked not only reduced total wages, but also impacted eligibility for benefits."[4]

Government estimates seem to track with real-life data in cities and states that have raised their minimum wage.

The University of Washington conducted a review of Seattle's increase of the minimum wage to $15, phased in over several years. Researchers wrote "those earning less than $19 an hour saw wages rise by 3.4% once the city's

---

[4] Research: When a higher minimum wage leads to lower compensation, by Qiuping Yu, Shawn Mankad and Masha Shunko, Harvard Business Review, June 10, 2021, available at https://hbr.org/2021/06/research-when-a-higher-minimum-wage-leads-to-lower-compensation

minimum wage was $13, while experiencing a 7.0%
decrease in hours worked."[5]

In other words, the hike was costing jobs. In fact, the
research showed there would be 5,000 more jobs in Seattle
if the hike had not been adopted.

While some businesses might be able to afford the hit of a
minimum wage hike, others will not. Restaurants, retail and
hospitality, for example, run on very low profit margins. The
impact there is likely to be much more severe.

Any minimum wage increase is particularly harmful to young
people. In Indiana, a $2.10 wage increase was followed by a
nearly eight percent decline in the number of 16- to 19-year-
old workers.[6]

VI.   Reduce wait times for building permits

Amid a housing shortage, permitting delays intensify scarcity
and add unneeded costs. Estimates show that delays in
permitting exceed six months and thousands of dollars in
many states. The Building Industry Association of Washington
estimates that the average building permit delay is 6.5
months costing homebuyers $35,000, and pricing thousands
of families out of the market.[7]

Similar results are seen across the country. The Wharton
Index from the University of Pennsylvania measures various
tactics of housing regulation in different counties across the
country (building permits are one of the regulatory hurdles
measured).[8] Three of the four mountain states are above the

[5] New evidence from the Seattle minimum wage study, Evans School of Public Policy &
Governance, the University of Washington, December 3, 2021, available at
https://evans.uw.edu/new-evidence-from-the-seattle-minimum-wage-study/
[6] Roll back the minimum wage, watch teens get jobs, by Michael Saltsman,
Employment Policies Institute, July 2010, available at
https://epionline.org/oped/o166/
[7] "Costs of Permitting Delays," BIAW, accessed on May 22, 2024, available at
https://www.biaw.com/research-center/cost-of-permitting-delays/
[8] "Measuring the Burden of Housing Regulation in Hawaii," University of Hawaii, April 14,
2022, available at https://uhero.hawaii.edu/wp-
content/uploads/2022/04/MeasuringTheBurdenOfHousingRegulationInHawaii.pdf

national average on the Wharton Index: Idaho, Montana, and Washington. Wyoming is below the national average.

Average Wharton Index by State
University of Pennsylvania

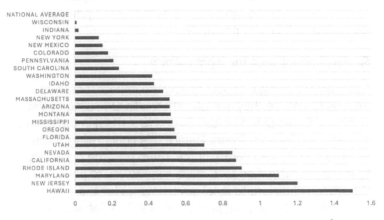

Success story from Florida

Florida was one of the first states to address building permit delays through bureaucratic penalties and building permit applications successfully increased. Florida House Bill 1059, signed into law in 2021 creates penalties for enforcement agencies if permits go unapproved within 30 business days for single-family units, or if additional information is not requested. A 10 percent reduction per day is then applied to the fee. 120 days is given for master building permit applications and the same 10 percent reduction per day is applied to the fee.

The new law is fixing the housing challenges in Florida. The Foundation for Government Accountability found that before the law was passed in October 2021, a suburb of Orlando processed less than half of the permit applications within 30 business days. After the law passed about 80 percent of applications were processed in 30 days. In Santa Rosa

County less than half were processed in 30 days before the law but after the law, the rate rose to 100 percent for 347 new homes. Housing permits have also grown by nearly half in some counties since October 2021.[9]

Policymakers should follow the successful example of Florida to reduce wait times by imposing bureaucratic penalties if permits aren't issued promptly.

VII.   Review impact fees for legal validity

Government officials should review the impact fees they impose to ensure they comply with the 2024 ruling by the Supreme Court of the United States (SCOTUS) in the case of *Sheetz v. El Dorado County.* Before this court ruling, if you wanted to build your family home, there was the possibility that impact mitigation fees could require you to pay thousands of dollars to local governments for the mere privilege of acquiring the proper permit. This fee was a preset figure by the legislature who believed it was exempt from proving the fees they were charging were reasonable. However, SCOTUS held in a unanimous decision that conditions placed on building permits are subject to heightened scrutiny and that fees must match the public's goals.[10]

The individual who brought this case, George Sheetz, argued that these impact mitigation fees violate the long-standing unconstitutional conditions doctrine, which, in sum, states the government cannot place a condition of receiving a public benefit on releasing a constitutional right. The Fifth Amendment to the U.S. Constitution provides more than the commonly known right to remain silent—it is also where a limit on the government's ability to take property without justly compensating the property owner can be found. This case

[9] "New Homes in Florida Are (Literally) Through the Roof Due to Permitting Reform," FGA, June 15, 2022, available at https://thefga.org/press/new-homes-in-florida-are-literally-through-the-roof-due-to-permitting-reform/

[10] "Court rules for property owner in building fee dispute," SCOTUS Blog, April 12, 2024, available at https://www.scotusblog.com/2024/04/court-rules-for-property-owner-in-building-fee-dispute/

arose because Mr. Sheetz wanted to use his land located in El Dorado County to its highest utility by building a home where he and his family could reside.

Sheetz sought a residential building permit from the defendant county, and while they obliged by providing a permit, it was on the condition he pay $23,420—a fee set by the state legislature to compensate for the alleged burdens the new construction would have on the county's traffic levels.

Court precedent on imposing impact fees

SCOTUS precedent, *Nollan* and *Dollan*, established the "essential nexus" and "rough proportionality" requirements between a permit fee imposed by a government body and the impact on the public. This means government bodies charging these types of fees should be required to prove the connection between the costs the individual homebuilder is incurring and what exactly the public is being compensated for.

These "impact fees" that Sheetz encountered are intended to mitigate the negative consequences of building in highly populated and wealthy areas. Proponents of the fees believe it to be a vital regulation tool to fund infrastructure such as schools, parks, libraries, etc. However, the impact fees, sometimes known as "exaction fees," quickly became a contested subject under the Fifth Amendment because builders, architects, and developers believed this to be an unduly burdensome barrier to performing work.

California is not the only place this practice has drawn controversy. Wyoming's impact fee schedules have also received backlash. Jackson and Teton counties have recently been scrutinized for their cost of building new homes and businesses. For instance, to build a 4,000-square-foot home in either of these quickly populating counties, the homebuilders incur $31,000 in fees demanded by the county. Due to Sheetz's success, these fees cannot be imposed unless the government can prove that this individual

Wyoming resident's building plan has a direct $31,000 impact on the public.

SCOTUS provided a narrow opinion. Justice Barrett, the author of the opinion said:

> "...there is no basis for affording property rights less protection in the hands of legislators than administrators. The Takings Clause applies equally to both — which means that it prohibits legislatures and agencies alike from imposing unconstitutional conditions on land-use permits."

Sheetz secured a win for property owners and builders across the country—governments are now subject to the two-part fairness test for the fees that they are imposing in the name of the public good. Public officials should ensure that they are complying with this ruling on impact fees and protecting important constitutional rights.

VIII.   Advance market options to improve housing affordability

Housing affordability and availability are major concerns in the Mountain West. Housing choices across the region have restricted and the area is one of the most *unattainable* in the nation. From 2018 to 2023, Idaho and Montana saw the largest home price increases in the nation at 74% and 72%, respectively. These higher costs leave many homebuyers in a lurch between high rental costs and growing down payment requirements.

What do the local and state governments do in this housing crisis? The answer is not a government solution but a market solution. Government track records in the area of housing affordability are very poor. Many of the so-called government fixes, like rent control, make housing more unaffordable.

Just look at Washington state. It is one of the most unattainable places to build or buy a home in the region and has held that position for many years, especially around the Seattle-metro area. All levels of Washington government have

created 'fixes' to the development problems facing the state. Limiting unwanted urban sprawl by severe growth management laws, protecting single-family residential zones from higher density housing, and pushing rent control and subsidized housing policies, to
name a few.

Breakdown of typical regulatory costs for building a home

Category	Regulations as a % of the house price
REGULATORY COST DURING LOT DEVELOPMENT	
Zoning approval	1.6
Compliance (fees, studies)	3
Land dedicated to government or otherwise left unbuilt	2.8
Standards, setbacks that go beyond ordinary	2.3
Complying with OSHA/other labor requirements	0.5
Pure cost of delay	0.4
All regulation during development	**10.5**
REGULATORY COST DURING CONSTRUCTION	
Fees paid by builder after purchasing lot	3.1
Changes in building codes	6.1
Architectural design standards beyond ordinary	2.7
Complying with OSHA/other labor requirements	1.1
Pure cost of delay	0.2
All regulation during construction	**13.3**
TOTAL COST OF REGULATION AS A % OF HOUSE PRICE	23.8

The result. Home costs just climbed higher. Why? Because not one of these solutions fixed the basic economic tenets of supply. If home supply goes up, prices go down. A variety of policies tailored to local needs must aim for more housing, not government band-aids on a supply issue.

Idaho, Montana, and Utah have always been more affordable than neighboring Washington, but in the last four years, this has shifted as new residents flock to these states. These states are unaffordable because demand has increased, but supply has not grown by the same magnitude.

The Mountain West region is one of few areas where it is cheaper to build a home rather than to buy a home, primarily in the more rural areas. Lower land costs and fewer regulations, make it cheaper for homebuyers to build rather than buy a typical single-family home. But this trend disappears in more urban neighborhoods because there are typically more regulations, development costs, and a tighter supply of construction labor. These are self-inflicted consequences of local government choices.

Housing regulatory and construction costs by state

State	Q3 2023 Median Home Price	Home Construction Cost	Regulatory Cost - Development	Regulatory Cost - Construction	Regulation total cost on home
Idaho	$368,260	$280,614	$38,667	$48,978	$87,645
Montana	$441,123	$335,136	$46,317	$58,669	$104,987
Washington	$457,450	$348,577	$48,032	$60,840	$108,873
Wyoming	$308,442	$235,032	$32,386	$41,022	$73,409
Oregon	$446,802	$340,463	$46,914	$59,424	$106,339
Utah	$494,239	$376,610	$51,895	$65,733	$117,628

How will the mountain states solve the housing crisis? The solution is allowing the market to supply houses.

Market options to improve affordability

The housing attainability crisis our region faces is not going to be fixed through government solutions and funding. The attainability crisis is an availability crisis and our local policies need to improve housing supply with the market, not the government. Improved housing supply will grant homebuyers more attainable choices.

Our region is expected to continue to increase in population, leaving the housing supply tight. Policies that favor increasing the housing supply are the best solution to increasing availability and affordability. Though often doubted, the simple theory of supply and demand applies to the housing industry. As the supply increases of houses, the prices decrease. State and local governments need to move away from Not In My Backyard (NIMB) policies that discourage denser housing and favor policies that make home building easier.

A few policies likely to increase the housing supply include:

- [ ] Light touch density development encourages multi-family residential building within previously single-family zones. LTD development can blend in with surrounding housing, provide a lower cost threshold to first-time home buyers, and increase supply in urban centers.

- [ ] Avoid restrictions on land development. Markets that are more highly regulated are also more expensive, as seen in Washington and Oregon. Growth should be permitted and encouraged in areas of poor agricultural production and low biodiversity. All levels of government should lower interference in the housing market and not restrict development unnecessarily.

- [ ] Enact policies shortening building permit timelines and limiting requirements, by financially incentivizing local government to comply. Florida adopted legislation that lowered building permit fees if deadlines were unmet. Since implementation counties once backlogged with permits, now issue permits quickly and within all deadlines.

- [ ] Simplify and minimize regulatory hurdles, incentivizing builders to enter the labor force. The contractor and property owner 'swarm' is an effective tool in meeting housing demands, because hundreds of small builders working on 1-3 units at a time, will build a lot more than one or two large builders building a hundred homes at a time.

- [ ] Avoid excessive energy code requirements for home building as this adds to the cost of the build and the complexity of the regulations. Washington state is changing energy code requirements for residential lots, and this will significantly increase home costs in coming years. It is estimated that costs have increased by almost $40,000 since 2009 from the WA State Energy Code Requirements.

In summary, policymakers should pursue policies that will improve housing supply including limiting building permit delays and complexity, encouraging light touch density development in highly demanded zones, not endangering property rights with growth management policies, avoiding excessive building mandates, and prohibiting artificial market manipulations like rent control and subsidies.

IX.   Provide constitutional protections for the Right to Work

Imagine going to work and being forced to pay a fee from every paycheck for a service you don't want. Frustration would be a mild reaction, outrage a more understandable one. Month after month, paycheck after paycheck, a portion of your wages would go to support a private organization you disagree with. This is the position many union members find themselves in across the country.

The First Amendment of the United States protects the rights of free speech and the courts have repeatedly affirmed this right naturally extends to freedom of association. Unfortunately, for workers in 24 states, because these states lack a right-to-work law, unions have found a workaround from the freedom of association.

Forced union membership is as undemocratic as it sounds. No American can be legally forced to join a formal union, but unions have historically found a way to protect their pocketbooks from uninterested members.[11] In non-right-to-work states, unions can require companies to charge 'non-member fees' as part of the employment conditions. These non-member fees are often the equivalent (or so close) to the member fee, that there is no point in opting out of membership.

---

[11] "Right to Work – What Is It, And More Importantly, What Isn't It?" Freedom Foundation May 8, 2018, available at https://www.freedomfoundation.com/labor/right-to-work-what-is-it-and-more-importantly-what-isnt-it/

Right to work vs. forced unionism states
As of 2024

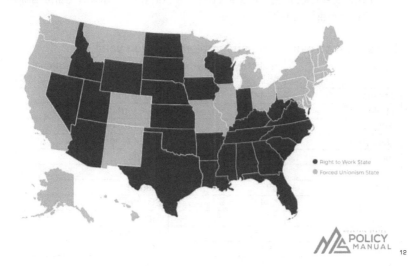

● Right to Work State
● Forced Unionism State

POLICY
MANUAL
12

A right-to-work law prevents these compulsory private membership practices. Instead of mandating that all workers in certain fields and careers must be members and pay the union dues, right-to-work states recognize that not all workers may agree with the practices of the unions. In right-to-work states, unions must *earn* the membership dues of their members. Guarding this protection within state constitutions is an important policy protection.

History of Right-To-Work

Right-to-work laws stem from the 1947 Taft-Hartley Act, Section 14B which prevented unions from requiring companies to fire workers who refused to join the union. After its passage, many states adopted right-to-work laws. In the last fifteen years, five states have also adopted the policy.

Idaho and Wyoming are right-to-work states that adopted their statutory protections decades ago. Wyoming became a

---

12 "Right to Work States Timeline," National Right to Work Committee, accessed on May 22, 2024, available at https://nrtwc.org/facts/state-right-to-work-timeline-2016/

right-to-work state in 1963 and Idaho in 1985. Unfortunately, for workers in Montana and Washington, they remain unprotected, and workers can be subject to union leadership they disagree with.

State right to work laws and implementation year

State	Right to work year	By statute or constitutional provision
Arkansas	1944	Constitution
Florida	1944	Constitution
Arizona	1946	Constitution
Nebraska	1946	Constitution
Virginia	1947	Statute
Tennessee	1947	Statute
North Carolina	1947	Statute
Georgia	1947	Statute
Iowa	1947	Statute
South Dakota	1947	Constitution
Texas	1947	Statute
North Dakota	1948	Statute
Nevada	1952	Statute
Alabama	1953	Statute, then Constitution
Mississippi	1954	Statute, then Constitution
South Carolina	1954	Statute
Utah	1955	Statute
Kansas	1958	Constitution
Wyoming	1963	Statute
Louisiana	1976	Statute
Idaho	1985	Statute
Oklahoma	2001	Constitution
Indiana	2012	Statute
Michigan	2013	Statute (repeal in 2024)
Wisconsin	2015	Statute
West Virginia	2016	Statute
Kentucky	2017	Statute

These laws create a balance between worker rights and union interests. No worker should be beholden to a private organization they disagree with to maintain employment. The propaganda against right-to-work stems from organized labor's fear of losing revenues based on compulsory membership. Union leadership argues that right-to-work destroys collective bargaining, decreases wages, increases poverty, and allows free riders. All of these are myths.[13]

☐ If collective bargaining is destroyed it is only the fault of the union not representing employees effectively. Effective unions will maintain their membership, whereas ineffective unions relying on compulsory membership and delivering poor service or questionable political activity will have earned their demise.

☐ Studies claiming lower wages and higher poverty questionably assume correlation is causation. Studies that dive deeper into the data and look at the cost-of-living assumptions turn these claims around and find that the rates do not vary significantly between right-to-work and non-right-to-work states. In fact, a recent Harvard Study found that people living in RTW areas have higher employment, higher labor force participation, lower disability receipts, and higher population growth because of the attractive economy. All these factors are associated with lower childhood poverty rates in RTW locations.[14]

☐ An interesting note is that a labor union's obligation to represent all employees (non-members too) is self-inflicted. If unions were willing to part with their hold on exclusive workplace representation, the free-rider argument would be pointless.

There is a big difference between public and private sector unions. As noted by President Franklin D. Roosevelt in this 1937 letter to the National Federation of Federal Employees:

"All Government employees should realize that the process of collective bargaining, as usually

---

[13] Ibid.
[14] "The Long-Run Effects of Right to Work," Harvard University, November 16, 2021, available at https://scholar.harvard.edu/files/matthew-lilley/files/long-effects-right-to-work.pdf

understood, cannot be transplanted into the public service. It has its distinct and insurmountable limitations when applied to public personnel management. The very nature and purposes of Government make it impossible for administrative officials to represent fully or to bind the employer in mutual discussions with Government employee organizations. The employer is the whole people, who speak by means of laws enacted by their representatives in Congress. Accordingly, administrative officials and employees alike are governed and guided, and in many instances restricted, by laws which establish policies, procedures, or rules in personnel matters. Particularly, I want to emphasize my conviction that militant tactics have no place in the functions of any organization of Government employees."[15]

Constitutional Amendment

There are 26 states protecting the fundamental rights of speech and association through right-to-work laws.[16] Of these 26 states, 10 have gone beyond statutory laws, protecting worker freedom directly in their state constitutions. Tennessee is the most recent state to vote for a constitutional amendment (2022), joining 9 other states with constitutional safeguards.

In November 2022, Amendment 1 won in all 95 counties in Tennessee and showed that workers want to be able to make their own choices concerning union membership.[17] Nearly 70

---

[15] "Letter on the Resolution of Federation of Federal Employees Against Strikes in Federal Service Online" The American Presidency Project, accessed on May 22, 2024, available at https://www.presidency.ucsb.edu/node/208681

[16] "Right to Work States Timeline," National Right to Work Committee, accessed on May 22, 2024, available at https://nrtwc.org/facts/state-right-to-work-timeline-2016/

[17] "Tennessee adds right-to-work to state constitution," Mackinac Center For Public Policy, November 9, 2022, available at https://www.mackinac.org/blog/2022/tennessee-adds-right-to-work-to-state-constitution

percent of Tennessee voters agreed with protecting the right to work in the state constitution.[18]

Amending the state constitution to include worker freedom, protects the existing right-to-work law from future political changes that would disadvantage workers to favor union leaders.

A strong right-to-work policy would add language to a state constitution making it unlawful for any person to be denied employment because they want to resign or refuse to join or affiliate with any labor union or employee organization. A benefit of right-to-work constitutional amendments is the opportunity for voters to cast their opinions. In Tennessee, voters agreed with the measure by a 2-1 margin showing how important freedom of association is to a majority of Americans.

Lawmakers in our region should put forward a right-to-work constitutional amendment and join the 10 other states with strong constitutional protections for workers and the economy.

---

[18] "Tennessee Constitutional Amendment 1, Right-to-Work Amendment (2022), BallotPedia, accessed on May 22, 2024, available at https://ballotpedia.org/Tennessee_Constitutional_Amendment_1,_Right-to-Work_Amendment_(2022)

I.   Require health care price transparency

America does not have a free market health care system and hasn't for the last 100 years. One needn't look further than the fact that a third party, either the government through insurance programs such as Medicare, Medicaid, and Obamacare, or employers through employee benefits pay for a very significant portion of health care in our current system.

The allocation of health care coverage in America
2022

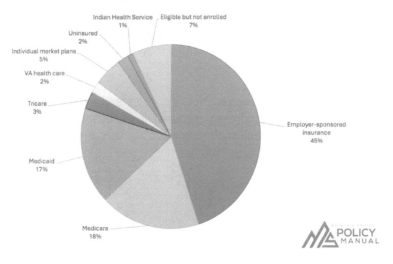

Consequently, until recently, prices in health care have not mattered to patients. Americans have been shielded from health care costs. Yet, insurance deductibles and out-of-pocket expenses have been increasing, putting more financial pressure on patients. The quality of "health care coverage" is often determined by the amount/cost an insurance plan covers, rather than the care itself.

Let's do a simple thought experiment. Pretend that every time you go to the grocery store there are no prices posted for the food products. You have no way of knowing how much anything costs until you get to the checkout counter. And when you do get to the check out, someone else pays for over 80 percent of your groceries.

On the one hand, you really don't care what prices are because someone else is paying for much of your food. On the other hand, you are still paying for a significant portion of your groceries, so it would be handy to know prices.

This thought experiment defines the current health care system in the United States.

Patients need details on the price of medical services

At the end of the day, health care is an economic activity, just like buying groceries, or clothes, or shelter. The relationship between a provider and a patient is unquestionably the most personal activity we undertake; however, health care has costs. The one thing that all policymakers can agree on is that the rising costs of health care are unsustainable. We currently spend almost 20 percent of our economy, or gross domestic product, on health care in the U.S. Unless something changes, this number is predicted to reach over 30 percent of GDP in the next 10 to 15 years.

To change this trajectory of increasing health care spending, price transparency is mandatory. Patients must have the ability to act as true consumers of medical care and be able to compare treatment prices from multiple providers. The federal government has mandated that hospitals publish their pricing structure, yet medical facilities have been extremely slow in meeting this requirement.

Here is the current timeline of price transparency efforts according to the American Enterprise Institute:[1]

---

[1] "Price Transparency 2.0: Helping Patients Identify and Select Providers of High-Value Medical Services," AEI, January 2023, available at https://www.aei.org/wp-content/uploads/2023/01/Price-Transparency-2.0.pdf?x85095

Timeline of health care price transparency efforts
American Enterprise Institute

March 2010	The Affordable Care Act is enacted. • Section 1001: Required posting of hospital charges • Section 1311(e)(3): "Transparency in Coverage"
August 2014	The Obama administration reminds hospitals of their obligation to make chargemaster rates available to interested parties.
August 2018	HHS finalizes the rule requiring hospitals to post chargemaster rates in a machine-readable format, starting in 2019.
November 2019	HHS finalizes the rule requiring hospitals to post chargemaster rates, negotiated rates, and prices for 300 shoppable services, starting in 2021.
November 2020	HHS finalizes the transparency in coverage rule for health insurers.
December 2020	The No Surprises Act is enacted. • Section 112: GFEs • Section 114: Maintenance of price comparison tool
January 2021	Hospital price transparency requirements go into effect.
July 2022	Health plan requirements for transparency in coverage go into effect (after a six-month delay).
January 2023	Health plans must post the pricing for 500 specified services and offer consumers an online tool for cost-sharing estimates. Medical services are obligated to produce GFEs for uninsured and cash-pay patients. (Enforcement is delayed for those with insurance.)
January 2024	Health plans must provide consumers with cost-sharing estimates for all services.

The first step in controlling health care costs is to give patients, as consumers of medical care, the ability to obtain quality care at the most reasonable price.

Competition in pricing is a fundamental of a free market and just as in grocery shopping, Americans should have the right to know prices for their medical care. Policymakers should work to require price details to be available to patients before services are provided.

II.   Make telemedicine permanent

The COVID-19 pandemic forced many health care providers to move their services online, and many Americans have enjoyed the benefit ever since. Unfortunately, Medicare beneficiaries and some privately insured patients could lose access to telemedicine by the end of 2024. This is because restrictions on telehealth were only temporarily waved by the federal government. Those waivers are set to expire unless Congress acts.

A 2021 survey found more than 23% of Americans have used telemedicine at least once over the past four weeks.[2] Studies have shown offering telehealth services can also dramatically lower the cost of care.

Several pieces of legislation are pending to make telemedicine permanent.[3] Policymakers should make sure to end this unnecessary restriction that can lower cost and improve access.

III.   Don't expand the Hospital 340B program without reforms first

As a safety net for the poor, Congress started a drug rebate program in Medicaid in 1990 to provide pharmaceuticals to the most vulnerable enrollees. Section 340B of the Public Health Service Act requires drug companies that participate in the Medicaid entitlement to sell outpatient pharmaceuticals to various medical facilities that provide care to low-income patients. The program began in 1992 and was essentially an extension of the original drug rebate plan.

Drug companies give outpatient medicines at a discounted price to facilities called "covered entities" that serve the poor or uninsured. However, covered entities can sell the drugs to anyone, not just the poor, regardless of their insurance or ability to pay.

In other words, these facilities obtain drugs at a mandated discount price through the 340B program, sell them at higher prices to insured and paying patients, and then collect the profits between the full retail price and their discounted price. The bottom line, the program has changed from assistance to the poor into a money-maker for these facilities

---

[2] Congress should take action to make telemedicine permanent, by Sally Pipes, May 20, 2024, available at https://www.sun-sentinel.com/2024/05/20/congress-should-take-action-to-make-telemedicine-permanent-opinion/

[3] Warner, colleagues push to preserve access to telehealth for seniors on Medicare, office of U.S. Senator Mark Warner, Virginia, January 23, 2024, available at https://www.warner.senate.gov/public/index.cfm/2024/1/warner-colleagues-push-to-preserve-access-to-telehealth-for-seniors-on-medicare

and an additional cost, or tax, for the drug manufacturers.

The definition of a covered entity has expanded several times since 1992, but Congress and newly passed laws, such as the Affordable Care Act, increased the number of qualified facilities dramatically. Obamacare added outpatient cancer clinics, rural clinics, sole community hospitals, and critical access hospitals to the list. Plus, the ACA increased Medicaid significantly.

340B program expanding but not serving the original goal

As of 2021, the 340B program accounted for 7.2 percent (approximately $44 billion) of all prescription drugs sold in the U.S. By 2022, the amount increased to $54 billion.[4] A total of 53,000 medical facilities participated in the 340B plan, which is almost double the number of facilities in the program in 2014.[5] The average profit margin on the sale of prescription drugs not obtained in the 340B program for medical facilities is 23 percent, compared to profits of 72 percent for drugs obtained in the 340B program.[6]

Over 40 percent of all insured patients in the United States are in the government programs of Medicare and Medicaid, both of which began in 1965. Since the 1980s, provider payments have gradually, but relentlessly, gone down. This has caused doctor and hospital consolidation so that medical providers could survive financially.

Unfortunately, medical facilities use the 340B program as another income source. Elected officials argue that the money comes from drug manufacturers and not taxpayers, so why not expand the program?

---

[4] "The 340B Drug Pricing Program," PHRMA, accessed on May 22, 2024, available at https://phrma.org/policy-issues/340b
[5] "Overview of the 340B Drug Discount Program," Congressional Research Services, October 14, 2022, available at https://crsreports.congress.gov/product/pdf/IF/IF12232
[6] "For-Profit Pharmacy Participation in the 340B Program," BRG, October 2020, available at https://media.thinkbrg.com/wp-content/uploads/2020/10/06150726/BRG-ForProfitPharmacyParticipation340B_2020.pdf

Although it began with the goal of helping the poor, the 340B program has morphed into a supplemental income plan for the participating medical facilities. The poor are not being helped as originally intended. The other untoward consequence of the program is the financial burden placed on the pharmaceutical manufacturers. Instead of more money for the research and development of life-extending and life-saving drugs, the companies are subsidizing medical facilities that the government can't financially support.

The 340B program either needs serious reform to actually support the most vulnerable patients or it should be closed. It definitely should not be expanded by policymakers in its present form.

IV. Reduce health insurance mandates to offer more insurance options

Americans view health insurance much differently than other types of insurance. When a person says that they have great health insurance, what they really mean is that their insurance covers a whole host of medical problems – eye wear, dental, preventive care, and routine check-ups. Other forms of insurance, for example homeowners, cover major problems, but routine issues, like mowing the lawn and cleaning the gutters are covered by out-of-pocket expenditures.

Compounding this difference between health insurance and other types of insurance are state and federal mandates that require policies to cover various medical problems. The Affordable Care Act, or Obamacare, requires every health insurance policy to contain ten specific mandates. Each state has its own mandates that in many cases overlap the federal mandates. As of several years ago, Wyoming had 32 health benefit and provider mandates, Montana had 31, and Idaho had 10.

Health care insurance benefit mandates by state

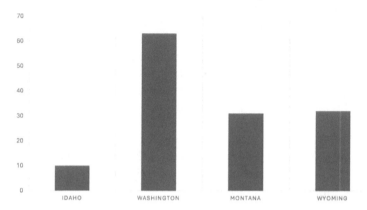

Instead of government-mandated "insurance" and entitlement programs that attempt to cover every possible health-related activity, health coverage needs to work like other forms of indemnity insurance used to mitigate risk, such as car, homeowners, and life insurance. Just as it makes little sense to use insurance to pay for gas or to mow the lawn, state and federal governments need to get away from the idea that health insurance should cover all our health-related events. True indemnity insurance should be there for catastrophes and emergencies. Routine day-to-day health services should be paid for out-of-pocket as needed.

Health mandates unnecessarily add cost

Each health care mandate increases the overall cost of health insurance. The reality is that not everyone needs all of the required mandates. For example, a healthy, unmarried thirty-year-old man does not need obstetrical coverage, yet he is paying for it in his health insurance plan. Women do not need tests to screen for prostate cancer.

Mandates are a classic example of politically powerful interest groups lobbying elected officials to include payment for their services in every insurance policy. Mandates restrict competition, drive up prices, and greatly restrict choices for patients.

Supporters of mandates say no one can predict a patient's future needs, so the government should require people by law to buy expensive coverage. It is true that the future is unknown, but a catastrophic, high-deductible insurance plan can be designed to cover any future major medical problem. Affordable auto and homeowner insurance policies, except in very unusual circumstances, cover any and all major problems and provide individuals and families with millions of dollars of coverage should the need arise.

As mentioned above, states vary in the number of mandates required. Unlike other forms of insurance, health insurance is sold on a state-by-state basis. A reasonable first step would be to allow the interstate purchase of health insurance. Patients would have a huge increase in their choices and the market would become much more competitive. The health coverage that some state governments mandate would still be available, but consumers would make their own decision about whether to buy it.

Americans across the political spectrum agree that the fundamental problem with health care in the United States is the ever-increasing cost. Reducing or eliminating government health insurance mandates altogether would be a definite move to lowering these costs.

V. **Abolish certificate of need (CON) requirements**

Limiting options is not a way to reduce cost or improve care.

Certificate of need (CON) laws are a state regulatory tool that seeks to limit the number of health care resources in a specific area under the theory that excess facilities will lead to excess cost. In fact, the opposite is true.

The United States Department of Health and Human Services has concluded that CON laws can restrict investments that would benefit consumers and lower costs in the long term and are likely to increase, rather than constrain, healthcare costs.[7]

Idaho and Wyoming do not have a CON law. Montana's CON requirement is limited to nursing homes. Washington state's CON requirement, which has been in place since 1971, is much more restrictive.[8]

As of January of 2020, health care services in Washington that needed a Certificate of Need included[9]:

- [ ] Ambulatory Surgical Centers (ASCs)
- [ ] Assisted Living & Residential Care Facilities
- [ ] Burn Care
- [ ] Cardiac Catheterization
- [ ] Home Health
- [ ] Hospice
- [ ] Hospital Beds (Acute, General Licensed, Med-Surg, etc.)
- [ ] Neonatal Intensive Care
- [ ] New Hospitals or Hospital-Sized Investments
- [ ] Nursing Home Beds / Long-Term Care Beds
- [ ] Obstetrics Services
- [ ] Open-Heart Surgery
- [ ] Organ Transplants
- [ ] Psychiatric Services
- [ ] Rehabilitation
- [ ] Renal Failure/Dialysis
- [ ] Substance/Drug Abuse

---

[7] Reforming America's Healthcare System through Choice and Competition, U.S. Department of Health and Human Services, 2017, available at https://ij.org/wp-content/uploads/2023/07/Reforming-Americas-Healthcare-System-Through-Choice-and-Competition.pdf

[8] National Conference of State Legislatures, Certificate of Need State Laws, Updated February 26, 2024, available at https://www.ncsl.org/health/certificate-of-need-state-laws

[9] Washington and Certificate of Need Programs, Mercatus Center, George Mason University, March 22, 2021, available at https://www.mercatus.org/publication/washington-and-certificate-need-programs-2020

☐ Swing Beds

Analysts at the Mercatus Center at George Mason University have found that there would be more health care services, as well as savings in the cost of healthcare spending in Washington state, if there were no Certificate of Need requirement.[10]

VI. Reject further Medicaid expansion

The passage of the Affordable Care Act, and the new, enticing dollars made available from the federal government convinced most states to expand their Medicaid coverage. In fact, all but nine states decided to take the plunge. Wyoming, wisely, decided against.

Medicaid expansion by state

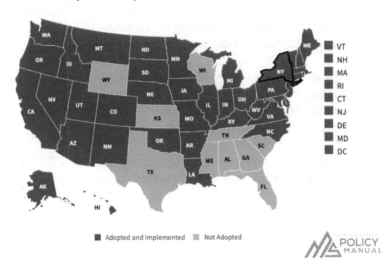

Adopted and Implemented ■ Not Adopted

Medicaid coverage can be extremely limiting, not only for patients but for health care facilities. Providers consistently run into billing problems, and reimbursement rates are so low that health care facilities will either limit the number of Medicaid patients or try to make up the cost elsewhere.

---

[10] Ibid

Medicare vs. Medicaid vs. private insurance reimbursements

Specialty	Medicaid Reimbursement	Medicare Reimbursement	Private Insurance Reimbursement
Total	74.3%	87.8%	96.1%
BROAD CATEGORIES			
Primary care	75.8	80.6	96.8
Surgical/medical care	72.9	93.8	95.5
SPECIFIC CATEGORIES			
Dermatology	46.2	97.7	98.0
General/family practice	76.0	93.6	94.0
General surgery	87.5	95.9	99.6
Internal medicine	62.9	95.2	98.8
Obstetrics and gynecology	81.7	88.7	98.9
Ophthalmology	77.4	-	-
Orthopedic surgery	85.8	99.1	99.2
Other specialties	70.0	92.8	96.0

In Montana, where Medicaid expansion happened in January of 2016, there has been a dramatic difference between hospital payments from Medicaid, and the cost of providing services to enrollees, according to the Foundation for Government Accountability.[11]

Hospital shortfalls before Medicaid expansion in the Treasure State totaled roughly $55 million. Post-expansion, hospital shortfalls are double at $110 million.[12] The data shows charity care has also fallen by nearly a third.

When Idaho voters passed Medicaid expansion in 2018, a lot of promises were made. Few, however, have panned out.

There were promises of limited enrollment – 60,000. But the latest numbers show more than double the projection and more than 1 in 4 Idahoans now enrolled.

There were promises it would be a good financial deal and lower health care costs. That hasn't happened either.

---

[11] Medicaid expansion deceives states and harms the truly needy, Foundation for Government Accountability, May 2024, available at https://thefga.org/research/medicaid-expansion-deceives-states/
[12] Ibid

The 2023 Idaho state budget increased Medicaid state spending to $856.3 million - a 25% increase from just four years ago. If the trend holds, Idaho will hit one billion dollars in Medicaid spending in the next few years.

As a Foundation for Government Accountability report indicates[13]:

> "In Idaho, there were at least 83,000 ineligible enrollees reported in January 2021. These enrollees do not meet traditional eligibility standards, but state officials are unable to remove them from the program because of the congressional handcuffs. If the trend continues, there could be hundreds of thousands of additional ineligible Medicaid enrollees. These ineligible enrollees would come with a monthly price tag of tens of millions of dollars—a figure that will only continue to grow as the public health emergency is prolonged."

Meantime, data from the Centers for Medicare and Medicaid Services shows the number of individuals enrolled on private insurance via the exchange has increased in the states that did *not* expand Medicaid. If they were to take the expansion plunge, at least 6,339 individuals in Wyoming would be forced on to the Medicaid rolls.[14]

How can lawmakers in Idaho, Montana and beyond begin to rectify the situation with Medicaid? By opting out of additional federal funding.

By removing the Medicaid handcuffs, policymakers can take control of their programs and focus on serving the most

---

[13] Shattered projections and broken promises, Foundation for Government Accountability, December 1, 2022, available at https://thefga.org/paper/able-bodied-adults-ineligible-enrollees-fueling-idahos-medicaid-surge/?fbclid=IwAR18PcGkOLp3nHgKc29vVm62ejcA4mi-qcU-oQkH6IYQBdhaAYL3VtzGXZo
[14] 2024 open enrollment period state-level public use file, U.S. Department of Health and Human Services, available at https://www.cms.gov/files/zip/2024-oep-state-level-public-use-file.zip

vulnerable populations, rather than being restricted by federal regulations. This would allow a state to tailor its Medicaid program to the unique needs of its residents and make more effective decisions about how to allocate resources. By prioritizing the truly needy, lawmakers can ensure that a Medicaid program is truly serving its intended purpose.

VII.   Expand the use and availability of Health Savings Accounts

Policymakers at the state and federal levels should be doing whatever they can to expand and promote the use of Health Savings Accounts (HSA's).

An HSA is an account that allows a user to set aside money on a pre-tax basis to pay for health care expenses. Often, employers will match an employee's contributions to an HSA. And, depending on how the HSA is setup, employees can earn interest in the account.

An HSA puts the power of everyday health care spending in the hands of the consumer. Instead of forcing citizens to abide by all the rules of their health insurance company, they can shop around and, in doing so, help put pressure on the market to lower costs and improve care. Current HSA account balances exceed $100 billion nationally roughly $3,000 per account, on average.[15]

Unfortunately, 90% of Americans lack access to health savings accounts. Why? Because, under current law, it is illegal to have an HSA unless you have a high-deductible health care plan. This means even those who are uninsured cannot legally save for their health care in an HSA. Most federal health care programs like Medicaid and Medicare don't meet the definition of high deductible, so Americans are shut out there as well.

---

[15] Why 90% of Americans lack access to health savings accounts, by Dean Clancey, Americans for Prosperity, October 2022, available at https://americansforprosperity.org/blog/how-to-fix-the-hsa-ceiling/

This makes no sense. Lawmakers can change the system by either decoupling HSA's from insurance altogether, or it could allow most insurance plans to be HSA-qualified.

One proposal recently introduced would even allow citizens to accept federal contributions to an HSA in lieu of reduced cost-sharing of insurance purchased through an exchange.[16]

For example, if a citizen buys health coverage through an exchange, cost-sharing by the federal government reduces the cost. Citizens would be able to choose whether they wanted a lower insurance premium, or a higher premium with the option to have an HSA partially funded by the government.

Researchers with the Paragon Health Institute contend doing so would result in approximately $1,400 a year being placed in a citizen's new health care savings account. For a younger adult who has few health care costs, the account could grow and be worth as much as $119,000 in 30 years.[17]

---

[16] The Access Act, introduced by Congressman Greg Steube and Congresswoman Kat Cammack, September 21, 2023, available at
https://steube.house.gov/uncategorized/steube-cammack-introduce-the-access-act/
[17] Follow the Money: How Tax Policy Shapes Health Care, Paragon Health Institute, available at https://paragoninstitute.org/private-health/follow-the-money-how-tax-policy-shapes-health-care/

I. **Use AI to improve government efficiency and save taxpayer money**

As Artificial Intelligence (AI) rapidly advances, state legislatures across the country are grappling with how to regulate this complex technology. States are taking diverse approaches, including cautious observation and proactive measures.

Many states, including Idaho, Washington, Montana, and Wyoming have tried to navigate this new territory. Here are steps policymakers can take to maximize the potential of AI while mitigating risks and ensuring financial value.

Identifying service inefficiencies

Before harnessing AI's power, state legislatures must first illuminate the area most ripe for improvement. This step demands an examination of government spending patterns. This includes a meticulous effort to analyze data on program costs, service delivery, and administrative functions across all departments. Here are areas that AI can help:

☐   Repetitive tasks: Are employees bogged down in manual data entry or paperwork? AI automation can free them for higher-value tasks.[1]

☐   Administrative bloat: Are layers of bureaucracy slowing down processes and inflating costs? AI can streamline workflows, reducing administrative overhead.[2]

---

[1] "3 Surprising Benefits of Artificial Intelligence in the Workplace," Beekeeper, March 1, 2024, available at https://www.beekeeper.io/blog/3-reasons-you-want-ai-in-the-workplace/

[2] "15 Ways Agencies Are Using AI To Streamline Workflows," Forbes, April 11, 2023, available at https://www.forbes.com/sites/forbesagencycouncil/2023/04/11/15-ways-agencies-are-using-ai-to-streamline-workflows/?sh=7ccf61d5d933

- ☐ Hidden inefficiencies: Analyze wait times for business filings, error rates, and citizen feedback to uncover hidden inefficiencies that drain resources.

Cost-benefit analysis to strike the balance between investment and savings

A rigorous cost-benefit analysis should be the cornerstone of any AI implementation plan. This analysis goes beyond simply accounting for the costs of developing, implementing, and maintaining AI solutions. It must meticulously estimate the potential cost savings generated by increased efficiency across various areas. One recent report by *Route Fifty* estimated AI could boost productivity by $519 billion a year across all U.S. governments.[3]

Percentage of companies reporting cost decreases from AI
McKinsey & Company

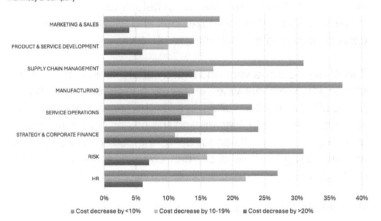

One example of a state using AI is the Robotic Process Automation (RPA) tool in Texas:

---

[3] "States look to AI for its potential to help with finances," Route Fifty, March 20, 2024, available at https://www.route-fifty.com/finance/2024/03/states-look-ai-its-potential-help-finances/395102/

"Texas uses RPA to collect data from the Bureau of Vital Statistics and Social Security Administration to compare against the eligibility system for a perfect match. The bot will automatically update the case to send a Notice of Adverse Action to one-person households that are reported deceased."[14]

Building a roadmap for phased implementation for sustainable success

Building a sustainable and successful AI implementation within state government requires a strategic, fiscally responsible approach. To have a successful implementation there must be a plan in place. Don't rush into widespread adoption. Instead, prioritize projects based on their potential for cost savings and efficiency gains. areas like repetitive tasks, data-driven decision-making, and fraud detection. Begin with low-risk pilot projects to test the water, gather valuable learnings, and refine the approach before wider implementation. This minimizes risk and allows for course correction based on real-world experience.

The AI landscape is vast and mostly unexplored in the public sector. It is likely that when implementing these practices, public officials will be trailblazers for the surrounding states and even the county. Harnessing the power of AI is not just about cost savings, it's about delivering better public services and improving the lives of citizens. By using a good process, public officials can effectively put AI to work for their state.

II.   **Protect the internet from misguided "net neutrality" efforts**

In 2015, the federal government adopted a policy that seemed to target a problem that didn't exist – "net neutrality." Net neutrality was supposed to prevent internet service providers (ISPs) from favoring or limiting internet traffic. It sounded good - in fact, large national companies and

---

4 "Use of Advanced Automation in SNAP," U.S. Department of Agriculture, January 10, 2024, available at https://www.fns.usda.gov/snap/advanced-automation

celebrities alike supported the idea - and predicted doom and gloom when it was repealed by the Federal Communications Commission (FCC) in 2017.

The problem is it was a heavy-handed, government regulatory approach that stifled competition and the freedom of the internet. And, to the extent that there was any issue in the first place, it would have been better dealt with using current laws that enforce competition.

Data shows that internet speed was improving before 2015 (pre-net neutrality) and continues to increase in this post-net neutrality world. Average broadband speeds in the United States have increased dramatically over the past six years. Average mobile internet speeds are up more than 300%.

Average broadband speeds by year

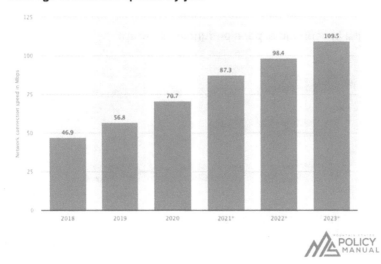

There have been very few - if any - examples of ISPs blocking content since net neutrality was repealed. Unfortunately, the biggest factor that determines your internet speed is the place you live. Typically, more rural areas experience slower internet speeds. This is why we need more innovation - and less regulation - to expand and improve access. Policymakers should avoid misguided efforts to impose "net neutrality" and instead focus efforts to expand access to high-speed internet.

III.   **Expand broadband coverage in a responsible way**

In today's rapidly evolving economic landscape, access to high-speed internet is critical for small businesses and education opportunities. As part of the Infrastructure Investment Bill and American Jobs Act (IIJA), passed in 2021, states are being provided billions of dollars by the federal government to help expand broadband.

For example, Idaho will have a big opportunity to expand broadband the right way with $583 million in federal funding. Neighboring states are also receiving substantial federal broadband funding with Washington state being allocated $1.2 billion, Montana $629 million, and Wyoming $348 million.

Federal broadband expansion funding by state

As policymakers utilize these federal funds, they should focus on best practices to ensure they are taking a free-market approach that expands broadband to the greatest number of people in the most efficient way possible.

Why broadband expansion is important

Broadband expansion refers to efforts aimed at increasing the availability and accessibility of high-speed broadband internet services in areas where they are currently limited or unavailable. It involves extending the reach of broadband infrastructure to reach more communities, homes, and businesses. Broadband expansion is critical for several reasons:

- Digital accessibility: It ensures more people have access to the internet, bridging the digital divide. Without broadband access, individuals and communities can be left behind in terms of education, employment, healthcare, and civic engagement.

- Economic development: Broadband expansion is seen as a driver of economic growth. It enables businesses to reach broader markets, facilitates remote work, and attracts investments in underserved regions.

- Education: Access to broadband is crucial for remote learning and education choice options, especially living in a post-COVID-19 world. According to the Federal Communications Commission, "Nearly 17 million school children lack internet access at home."

- Healthcare: Telehealth and remote healthcare services rely on broadband access. Expanding broadband can improve healthcare access, especially in rural and remote areas.

- Government services: Many government services and information are now provided online. Broadband expansion ensures citizens can access government services efficiently.

Five steps for successful broadband expansion

To help ensure a successful broadband expansion implementation, policymakers should follow these five steps:

- ☐ *Step one: Understand your market.* Broadband, with its high-speed internet capabilities, has become an indispensable tool, weaving its way into the very fabric of our daily lives and operations. Engaging industry experts can provide invaluable insights into the latest advancements, challenges, and the promising future of broadband.

- ☐ *Step two: Find the right projects.* State and local gove rnments often rely on comprehensive broadband mapping. These maps, developed in collaboration with the FCC or independent organizations, provide detailed insights into areas lacking adequate broadband access. For instance, Idaho's Broadband Task Force has been instrumental in identifying underserved regions, guiding the state's efforts in bridging the digital divide.

- ☐ *Step three: Maximize investments.* Traditional fiber optic networks, while effective, have been found to not always be the most cost-efficient solution for remote areas. Exploring alternative technologies, such as fixed wireless, satellite internet, or low-power wide-area networks, can offer more economical solutions for challenging terrains or low-density regions. Companies like SpaceX's Starlink are aiming to provide broadband access via low-Earth orbit satellites. This could be a game-changer for remote and underserved areas.

- ☐ *Step four: Don't treat federal suggestions as mandatory.* While federal guidelines are designed to ensure a uniform approach to broadband expansion, local legislators and implementers need to know they have the strategic autonomy to adapt these suggestions to the community's specific needs. A one-size-fits-all policy may not suit the diverse landscapes and demographic nuances of different regions. It is important to remember that federal guidance should serve as a starting point for collaboration rather than a checklist for compliance. For example, in response to a question about requiring a union workforce to expand broadband, Idaho told the federal government: "The IOB has opted not to require applicants to have a unionized workforce."

☐ *Step five: Limit government overreach.* Excessive and cumbersome regulations can act as deterrents, hindering private initiative and inflating project costs. By simplifying regulatory frameworks and ensuring transparent, competitive bidding processes, local governments can pave the way for efficient and equitable broadband projects. Such measures not only make it more attractive for private companies to participate but also guard against potential government favoritism, ensuring a level playing field. Collaborations with utility companies to utilize existing poles, conduits, or even public buildings can significantly reduce project costs. Governments should not attempt to create their own broadband utilities or institute price caps.

Policymakers now have a generational opportunity to expand high-speed internet in their states with federal broadband funds to help improve digital accessibility, economic development, education opportunities, healthcare access, and government services. By focusing on these five steps government officials will be able to ensure a successful and cost-effective broadband expansion implementation in their states.

IV. Be wary of constitutionally suspect content filter policies

Deciding when to let your child jump into that tech world is not easy. No matter how many rules your family may have, it is still natural to worry about what your children will find, or who they'll talk to, online. It has been more than a quarter century since Congress passed a law to protect kids online. In 1998, less than half the country was even connected to the internet, and those who were likely used AOL. There was no Facebook. There was no social media.

Today, more than half of teenagers say it would be difficult to give up their social media time, according to Pew Research polling. Half of parents are worried about what their child is being exposed to online. Social media and the internet are very much mobile. It would be nearly impossible for companies to create 50 different oversight mechanisms to comply with every state's preference. And even if they did, teens and families move fluidly across state lines. A patchwork of laws would mean they are inconsistently protected.

Several state-specific restrictions have run afoul of the constitution

Some state efforts to protect children online have pointed to laws recently passed in Utah and Arkansas to restrict social media access. Both states created significant legal liability for certain types of content, mandated internet users hand over their sensitive, private data to confirm their identities, and in Utah's case, required certain internet services to be shut off every evening.

While these efforts were well-intentioned, all these bills have invited enormous legal scrutiny. For example, Utah, Arkansas, Ohio and California were all sued, and lost.

In Arkansas, U.S. District Court Judge Timothy Brooks agreed the legislation was an unacceptable affront to free speech, saying that the "loss of First Amendment freedoms, even for minimal periods of time, constitute[s] irreparable injury," and that there was "no compelling evidence" that children would be protected by the legislation.[5]

---

[5] NetChoice, LLC vs. Tim Griffin, United States District Court Western Division of Arkansas, August 31, 2023

A judge in California took the state to task for claiming their speech regulation bill would somehow improve children's privacy. Judge Beth Labson Freeman said that age verification mandates are "likely to exacerbate the problem by inducing...children to divulge additional personal information."[6] Every time these bills have been challenged, they have failed to withstand even basic constitutional scrutiny.

Censorship regimes like this were attempted before at the federal level in 1996 and struck down by the U.S. Supreme Court as unconstitutional.[7] There is no reason to believe that this time would be any different.

Ensuring our children are safe online is of critical importance. No sane person denies this. But an important question for every American to ask themselves is: Have I made my child safer by weakening their constitutional rights and empowering the government to be my co-parent? The answer is clearly not.

Tech companies have introduced various ideas to help with the effort as well. But it should be noted that filters, blockers, and screen time monitors already exist and don't come with draconian government mandates. States like Florida are implementing digital literacy and safety into school curricula.[8]

Improving outcomes for children and keeping them safe online requires work–work that is worth doing. But it is important that the efforts lawmakers undertake lead us to our desired outcomes. Passing a bill that will inevitably be struck down as violating the First Amendment won't make a single child safer. Instead, policymakers need to do the hard work of finding policy solutions that place the family, not the government, at the center of a child's upbringing, and give them safety tools they can use free of government coercion or censorship.

---

[6] Ibid
[7] "Reno v. ACLU," Columbia University, June 26, 1997, available at
https://globalfreedomofexpression.columbia.edu/cases/reno-v-aclu-2/
[8] "HB 379 – 2023," Florida Legislature, available at
https://www.flsenate.gov/Session/Bill/2023/379/BillText/er/PDF

Meanwhile, Congress needs to work with tech providers to create a standard for the national marketplace to ensure uniform protection for kids' online health and safety.

Can protection start at the app store?

One idea put forward by Meta – the parent company of Facebook – is to require parental consent for teens under 16 at the app store level. What does this mean?

Essentially, parents would have to approve any download of an app other than general items such as search or email. Age verification would be completed at the app store level – which would ensure kids are placed in the appropriate app experience. All apps would need to be treated consistently.

Another proposal would require ad targeting standards that would limit the personalization of ads to those under 16 to age and location only. This means advertisers and videos that may be questionable could not be targeted to kids under 16.

These are common sense proposals that recognize the complexity of the issue. There will likely be many more ideas on the way.

Policymakers can protect kids online while not stifling innovation and advancement in the coming years. A patchwork of laws is messy. One national standard that puts parents, not the government, in the driver's seat, would be best.

I. **Minimize the regulatory burden imposed on farmers**

Agriculture is a pivotal industry to the Mountain States, contributing billions of dollars annually. Jobs and businesses depend on the success of farmers and ranchers, but challenges are increasing for the region's agribusinesses. Inflation is challenging farmers nationally and regulatory pressure is increasing as West Coast politicians push for more restrictive laws.

To help facilitate a favorable climate for farmers to excel, policymakers should embrace free-market agricultural policies. This focus would move the legislative needle toward more farm independence and improved food self-reliance. As more farms thrive by relying on ingenuity and grit to move products to markets, individuals can more easily meet food needs with affordable and secure food.

Agriculture relies on many limited resources, including water, land, minerals/oil, and labor. The limitations of these resources exist naturally and yet man-made limitations, in the form of regulations, add to the difficulty of procuring a sufficient supply of inputs.

Regulations tighten the supply of all inputs needed for agriculture, naturally limited resources or otherwise (i.e., technology, trade, research, marketing, transportation, and financial). Increasing regulatory burdens on agriculturalists will consolidate domestic farming operations and agricultural businesses, endangering an accessible and affordable food supply.

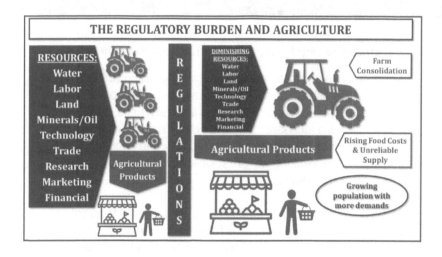

Resource availability and restrictions

Policies affecting agriculture at the federal, state, and local levels should seek to remove restrictions on these resources. Agricultural regulations often affect the availability and accessibility of resources. For example, policy efforts to increase agricultural water supply make more available for use. Other regulations can affect accessibility to existing water, such as clean water legislation and salmon protections.

Historically, government efforts have placed great emphasis on increasing the availability of resources to agriculture. Dam construction, land allotments, and research funding propelled American agriculture to its current standing. Free market policy encourages government funding or research and infrastructure and public/private partnerships in projects. In recent years, agriculture's ability to develop resources and continue using existing resources has often been opposed by special interests and bureaucracy. Some positions even advocate for the removal of available resources, including the Snake River dams.

Policies should allow for the advancement of free markets first, spurring development and use of these resources by private sources and/or private/public partnerships, in a fair balance with conservation and economic needs. Recent efforts to change farm policies have tightened accessibility.

Environmental regulations, diverting land to national protection, and limiting well and oil drilling are all examples of preventing access to resources. Regulatory positions need to carefully assess the benefit of resources to farmers and the food supply against the costs often alleged by special interest groups. Some protection of resources captures externalities and is worth the resource limitations because the benefit to the communities outweighs the costs to agriculture and food supply. However, many regulations move far beyond scientific criteria, preventing access to resources because of the interests of a few, at the cost of a food supply that feeds many.

Regulations interfering with the ability to farm must consider the actual cost and impact on farmers, farmworkers, and communities. Regulations favoring one individual's story over a community's experience are damaging to agricultural businesses, rural families, and towns.

II. **Protect agricultural water uses and the development of water storage**

Clean water is essential, but unnecessary and unscientific restrictions on water use need to be removed. Farmers should have the ability to access water and help fund additional water expansion projects via usage fees. States need to respectfully balance water for agricultural use and reasonable fish recovery efforts.

Across the western states, the use it or lose it water laws discourage water conservation. States need to encourage water conservation, and not unduly punish farmers for adopting efficient technologies and conserving water resources. Individual farmers and canal companies would benefit from legislation that encourages conservation, without losing their existing water rights.[1]

Water is for fighting and whiskey is for drinking, is an old western phrase still holding true today. Across the western United States prior appropriation doctrine, the idea that first in time is first in right rules the water law, but what happens when this water starts disappearing? The fairness of making the most junior rights disappear before senior rights adopt any conservation strategy is not only selfish but also poor environmentalism. Instead, state-level policies should look at adopting groundwater conservation easements to protect aquifers.

State-level policies can change to create a market-based tool that would incentivize water users to voluntarily stop pumping from groundwater resources in exchange for direct payments or tax benefits. These are permanent, voluntary, and specific to the land parcels and they can serve as a tool to recover depleting aquifers in the Mountain States.

III.   **Balance land development and property rights with the necessity of land for food production**

Property rights must be protected. However, tax exemptions on agricultural land should account for changes in use, encouraging farmers to slow the development of agricultural land for housing purposes. Local and state policies already influence the decision through property taxes. Using the existing exemptions to encourage farmers to protect agricultural land is a free market method of protecting farm ground.

Policies should balance the right of the farmers to lease their land for the best available use. Undeveloped land should be made accessible for agricultural land developers and for housing and commercial development to decrease the

---

[1] Western water strategy shifting from 'use it or lose it,' to 'waste not, want not', The Hill, June 2018, available at https://thehill.com/opinion/energy-environment/392341-western-water-strategy-shifting-from-use-it-or-lose-it-to-waste

pressure for farm ground conversion. The growing population of the western states has increased the conversion of farmland to subdivisions and commercial properties.

Where once sprawled thousands of acres of farmland, housing developments are covering the landscape and decreasing farming in many regions. Most regions give property tax exemptions to agricultural land and local communities can use property tax incentives to discourage urban sprawl and encourage farmland preservation. A policy in this directive should carefully weigh strategies.

Transfer of Development Rights (TDRs) is another policy option for balancing housing supply and agricultural land protection. TDRs are local policy tools available to counties, allowing density to remain concentrated around population centers and compensating farmers for their land's development rights. TDRs can be adopted by local governments, allowing a market to be created for the right to develop ground. This policy would alleviate the housing shortage and protect agricultural ground at the same time. TDRs are designed differently across the nation, but some key requirements would include:

- ☐ Specific development goals and designated areas of sending and receiving TDRs.

- ☐ TDRs should be restricted to housing development.

- ☐ Formalize inter-jurisdictional agreements between counties and municipalities for the handling of TDRs.

- ☐ Create a market for development rights with open and transparent historical pricing but avoid government-run TDR banks.

- ☐ Limit government regulation of TDRs.

IV.   Agricultural labor needs to be accessible

A recent study by Texas A&M found, that when farmers can't hire workers, expect to see a continued rise in inflation, increasing food prices, and more empty shelves at the grocery store.[2] That study sets aside immigration as a much larger federal issue and focuses on state efforts impacting the ag workforce. Less regulations, lower taxation, and avoiding agricultural overtime mandates will help farmers and ag businesses find and keep these valuable employees, which makes harvest successful.

Family and hired farmworkers on U.S. farms

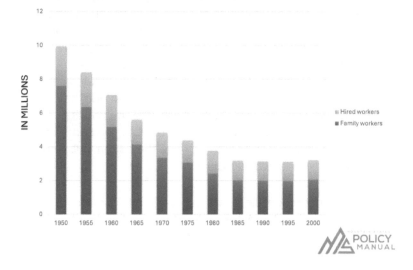

The shortage of agricultural labor is nothing new. Pre- and post-pandemic, farms struggled to find willing workers. From 1950 to 2000, hired farmworkers declined by 52% and family farmworkers declined by 73%.[3] The stressful and strenuous nature of the job, volatility of commodity prices, high start-up costs, and immigration all contribute to fewer

---

[2] "The Link Between Consumer Prices, Labor Costs, and Immigration in the U.S.: Bivariate Associations," Texas A&M University, available at
https://www.tamiu.edu/coas/documents/tamiu-abic.pdf
[3] "The U.S. Farm Labor Shortage," AG AMERICA, February 26, 2020, available at
https://agamerica.com/blog/the-impact-of-the-farm-labor-shortage/

farmworkers. State efforts can also negatively impact the employment environment, as in the case of Washington.

Washington far outranks Montana, Idaho, Utah, and Wyoming in their number of agricultural workers. Unfortunately for Washington farmers, their state burdens them with more complications. Washington state requires multiple layers of regulation to hire H-2A workers, wastes tax dollars to hire uninterested local workers, and recently removed the agricultural overtime exemption. From 2002 to 2017, Washington saw the 2nd highest loss of agricultural employers in the nation, a 23% decrease.

Oregon, following Washington's lead, has enacted challenging agriculture labor legislation. The result urged some farms along the border to jump ship and move packing houses to the more friendly state of Idaho. Or even more sadly, small family farms gave up and the ground has been taken over by larger corporations that can more efficiently handle the staffing complexities. From 2002-2017, Oregon experienced a 6% loss in operations hiring workers, while Idaho increased its farm operations by 3%.

H-2A (temporary visa) workers are vital to farms

Excessive state restrictions on the H-2A program need to be stopped due to the damage to an already complex and frustrating system. Bureaucratic delays in paperwork, excessive housing and work environment requirements, unrealistic efforts to encourage the employment of domestic workers, prevent and postpone H-2A workers from working and receiving a good income to take back home.

Agriculture labor needs will always be seasonal, and laws should favor workers that adapt and thrive in this seasonality. Laws that complicate the ability to pay workers based on performance (i.e., piece-rate pay) or that prevent workers from earning a year's income in a 6-9 month season (i.e., agricultural overtime) hurt farmworkers and farmers. Agriculture's long-existing overtime exemption has been removed in California, Washington, Oregon, and other states.

The implementation of this policy is quickly eroding the ability of workers to earn a year's income within the 6-9 month growing season and for farms to meet the seasonal labor demands of farming.

V. Taxes should not unfairly favor or punish farmers

Farmers should be treated equally with other businesses. Taxes need to respect how agri-businesses are organized, and not unduly burden farming organizations. The federal government's so-called 'Death Tax' can destroy farming operations.

When someone dies without effective estate planning, the federal government will claim up to 40 percent of the value of the taxable estate. For farmers, who are land rich but cash poor, the liquid assets needed to cover the taxable value are insufficient. Farms are then sold to pay the debt. Legislators have increased the exemption amount in recent years and are working on making this fix more permanent. States without death taxes should avoid one and those with them should repeal them.

VI. Protect the ability of small farms to thrive

Farm numbers across the United States are dwindling and our region is no exception. Our country lost 7% of farms from 2017 to 2022, and all of the Mountain States were above the national average.

From 2017 to 2022, Idaho, Montana, Washington, and Wyoming all experienced a decrease in the total number of farms. Wyoming saw the largest decrease at 12% of farms, totaling 1,394 farms in the state that chose to end operations. Montana and Washington had the second largest decreases of 10 percent, a raw total of 2,782 and 3,717 farms, respectively. Idaho trailed behind at 8 percent with 2,119 farms ending operations.

Total loss of farms
2017-2022

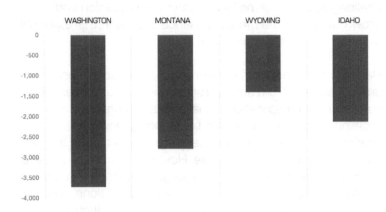

The decrease in farms over the last five years is the largest seen between two National Agricultural Censuses. This decrease in farming operations is seen despite the highest net farm income recorded during this time frame.

Why, during a period of historical profits were farms ending operations?

According to the census data in 2022 and 2017, farm losses were highest in the low-income categories. The smaller farms are the ones disappearing at upwards of 40% and close to 50% in the case of Idaho farms with incomes between $200,000 to $499,999. Farm number losses are huge for operations under half a million dollars in total sales.

But the trend reverses for farms with revenue above $500,000. Almost all income brackets above $500,000 saw an increase in farming operations (except one income bracket in Montana). With the largest increases in the top income category of $10,000,000 or more.

The loss of farms isn't driven by only one issue. Regulations, input costs, pandemic changes, trade disruptions, aging operators, and agricultural land development are all pushing out farms. The smallest farms are experiencing the greatest challenges. Some farms have risen to the occasion and grown to survive the market variance. However, there are still many farms ending operations.

Having many producers involved in food production insulates end consumers from supply disruptions. One producer will likely experience operational challenges throughout the growing season be it weather, trade, policy, or labor challenges. If only a few producers are present in the market supply disruptions are inevitable. However, if many producers, both small and large, are actively engaged in the industry, it insulates the end consumer from supply disruptions, because it is unlikely many producers face the same production challenges.

U.S. farm income is falling
January 2022

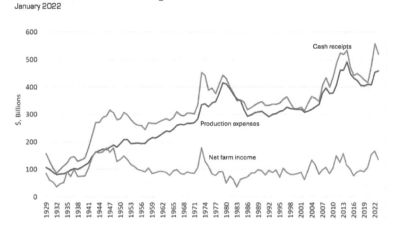

Challenges are increasing for farm operations as this last year was expected to be one of the largest declines in net cash farm income in history, the largest in nominal terms, and third largest adjusted to inflation.[4] Farms need to become resilient to market fluctuations like the one experienced in 2023.

Efforts should be made to ease the burdens of remaining in the agricultural industry for small producers like decreasing regulatory burdens, encouraging agricultural land to remain in production at reasonable rental rates, improving labor supply restrictions, and encouraging trade agreements benefiting agricultural products. Before policies are adopted it is worth questioning what the result will be for small producers, because those are the operations least likely to survive.

---

[4] "USDA Forecasts Sharpest Decline in U.S. Farm Income in History," U.S. Senate Committee On Agriculture, Nutrition & Forestry, September 7, 2023, available at https://www.agriculture.senate.gov/newsroom/minority-blog/usda-forecasts-sharpest-decline-in-us-farm-income-in-history

I. Protect the numerous benefits of the Snake River dams

In an era of electrification and increased power demand, it makes no sense to remove a clean, renewable power source. Hydropower is an important source of reliable and clean energy for everyone in the Northwest. The lower Snake River Dams are critical to the infrastructure of the region, providing not only power benefits but also reductions in flood risk, crop irrigation, barging, and much more.

Unlike intermittent wind and solar power, the Snake River dams provide more than 1,000 average megawatts of reliable baseload, carbon-free energy that can be turned on at any moment. That's enough energy for over 800,000 average U.S. homes.

Removing the Snake River dams would have serious negative regional impacts

The federal government undertook a multi-year public process in 2020 to produce a comprehensive review of the issues surrounding the Snake River dams and possible breaching. Here are some of the findings from that study:[1]

☐ "[Dam breaching] would not meet the objective to Provide a Reliable and Economic Power Supply . . . The lower Snake River projects provide more than 2,000 MW of sustained peaking capabilities during the winter, and a quarter of the federal power system's current reserves holding capability. The dams play an important role in maintaining reliability in the production of power used to supply load in the Pacific Northwest. Their flexibility and dispatchability are valuable components of the CRS. [Dam breaching]

---

[1] "Executive Summary - Columbia River System Operations Environmental Impact Statement," U.S. Army Corps of Engineers, Bureau of Reclamation and Bonneville Power Administration, available at
https://usace.contentdm.oclc.org/utils/getfile/collection/p16021coll7/id/14957

would more than double the region's risk of power shortages..."

☐ "The costs of an expanded zero-carbon resource portfolio designed to replace the full capability of the four lower Snake River dams would be significant: up to twice the $400 million assumed to maintain regional reliability. Additional variables such as resource financing uncertainties and the uncertainty in the cost and availability of demand response add to this rate sensitivity. If Bonneville had to replace the four lower Snake River projects' full capability with zero-carbon resources, the rate pressure could be up to 50% on wholesale power rates."

☐ "The lower Snake River shallow draft navigation channel would no longer be available, eliminating commercial navigation to multiple port facilities on the lower Snake River... As a result, the cost to transport goods to market would increase."

☐ "Under this scenario, increases in vehicular accident rates, highway traffic and congestion would occur. In addition, additional wear and tear on roadways could result in additional road repair costs of up to $10 million annually."

☐ "Farmers could also experience increased production costs associated with higher transportation costs for upriver movements (i.e., fertilizer, crops). There would be additional demands on existing road and rail infrastructure as well as at barging facilities near the Tri-Cities, Washington, increasing traffic and air pollution."

☐ "Adverse regional economic effects would occur as the jobs and income provided by the four primary commercial navigation ports would be curtailed, including the Port of Lewiston, the Port of Clarkston, the Port of Whitman County (Wilma, Almota, Central

Ferry), and the Port of Garfield."

☐ "Despite the major benefits to fish expected from [dam breaching], this alternative was not identified as the Preferred Alternative due to the adverse impacts to other resources such as transportation, power reliability and affordability, and greenhouse gas emissions."

Baseload power is needed to counter the unreliability of intermittent power sources like wind and solar

Among the many benefits of the Snake River dams is the reliable baseload power provided. This is critical when the energy system is stressed during periods of extreme cold or heat. The 2023 Winter was a great case study for the reliability problem of intermittent green sources like wind and solar that are being pushed nationwide. Consider the following examples from Montana and Washington.

In Montana, Northwestern Energy spokesperson Jo Dee Black commented, "Wind and solar generation could not produce much if any, power during the extreme cold."[2]

In Washington, Grant County PUD stated, "frigid temperatures throughout Grant County and the Pacific Northwest pushed energy use to record levels, strained many regional electric grids, and put a heavy draw on our region's capacity to generate electricity."[3]

The same problem occurs during periods of extreme heat. Wind and solar intermittent energy sources are not reliable. Wind specifically disappears when there are extremely high or low temperatures. This is why it is critical to have reliable

[2] "Cold snap fuels Montana's coal power debate," Montana Freepress, January 22, 2024, available at https://montanafreepress.org/2024/01/22/cold-snap-fuels-montanas-coal-power-debate/
[3] "Arctic blast flashes warning signal for regional grid stability and reliance on intermittent power sources," Mountain States Policy Center, January 24, 2024, available at https://www.mountainstatespolicy.org/cold-snap-flashes-warning-signal-for-regional-grid-stability-and-reliance-on-intermittent-power-sour

baseload power sources to pick up the slack when energy demand is high to avoid blackouts.

State power portfolios
As of 2024

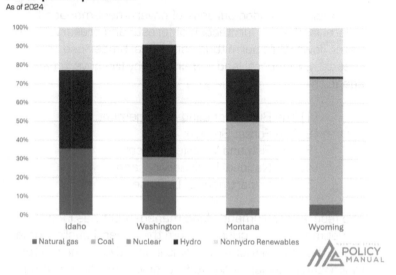

Diversification efforts of the power grid are a worthy goal if they don't come at the expense of reliable baseload power. When families try to stay warm during an arctic blast or try to stay cool during extreme heat, policymakers need to make sure the power is reliably and economically available for them.

As states navigate the complexities of the energy transition, sustainability, and affordability, they must be wary of using intermittent sources to replace reliable baseload power such as the energy and other economic benefits provided by the Snake River dams.

II.   **Work to restore more state control over federal land**

Federal land is defined as land that is owned by the United States federal government. The Property Clause in Article 4 Section 3 of the United States Constitution gives the federal government the right to manage and purchase land and regulate the activities that take place on that land.

The federal government owns approximately 640 million acres of federal land, which comprises about 28% of the 2.27 billion total acres of land in the United States.

The original, intended purpose of government-managed federal land is the "protection of forests and preservation of water flows while permitting some local timber use." Presently, all federal land is managed by five government agencies:

(1) The Bureau of Land Management;
(2) The Forest Service;
(3) The Fish and Wildlife Service;
(4) The National Park Service; and
(5) The Department of Defense.

The federal government's land management has faced sometimes intense criticism from the general public. Some argue the federal management is ineffective, some say too much land is owned by the federal government, and some contend the land has economic benefits and should be returned to private citizens.

States with the highest percentage of public land

State	Federal %	State %	Total
Alaska	61.0%	34.8%	95.8%
Nevada	80.1%	7.7%	87.8%
Utah	63.1%	12.1%	75.2%
Idaho	62.9%	7.5%	70.4%

III.   Demand higher federal PILT reimbursements

One way the federal government attempts to mitigate potential losses in economic activity for states with large amounts of federal land is by compensating them with Payments in Lieu of Taxes, or "PILT." Since federal land is owned by the government and cannot be taxed, PILTs are a way that the federal government attempts to aid citizens living near federal land by giving each county a payment which is calculated based on the number of acres owned by the federal government and the county's population. The PILT approach is not necessarily the most effective because it does not take into consideration the amount of federal land in each county when determining how much to pay.

Because several counties with the highest amount of federal land are also rural and have lower populations, the amount they received in PILT does not reflect the amount of untaxable federal land within their borders. This system leaves rural counties struggling to provide public goods and services since they are unable to tax such a large portion of their territory, and the federal government fails to assist them in bridging that gap.

Another common criticism of the federal government's land ownership is that federal land is often managed ineffectively. The Bureau of Land Management has set a series of land-health standards which measure biological conditions on federal lands such as soil health, water quality, and the protection of endangered species. These standards must be maintained for the use of these federal lands to be sustainable.

However, the Public Employees for Environmental Responsibility (PEER) conducted a study on 21,000 allotments of federal land across several states and found that many assessed allotments failed to meet the Bureau of Land Management's health standards. These mismanaged areas were most commonly found in cold desert ecoregions and researchers there observed extreme temperature swings and a lack of moisture. PEER determined that the primary cause of this damage was livestock grazing on federal land. This sharp decline in land health is detrimental to the plants and animals that live within these territories and demonstrates a distinct failure on the part of the federal government to effectively manage and protect this land.

Improved economic outlook by moving federal land to state control

Finally, critics of federal land management argue that transferring ownership of federal land to the states would result in significant financial benefits. In states such as Idaho, where agriculture is a major industry and where the federal government owns two-thirds of the total land, concerns are raised about the large amounts of revenue that Idahoans lose, even though the federal government attempts to mitigate these potential losses through measures such as PILTs.

The Property and Environment Research Center (PERC) looked at the financial returns produced by federally-owned land, as well as state-owned land in four western states and found that these four states earned an average revenue of $14.51 for every dollar spent on state land management. This is in sharp contrast to the average of 73 cents earned for each dollar spent on federal land management – a whopping 95% lower. The study also compared the management of timber, grazing, minerals, and recreation by both state and federal governments and determined that state management of these industries can produce significantly higher revenue than the current system of federal management, which would greatly assist local economies.

There is significant evidence to suggest that states would benefit if the federal government transferred some of this land to local control. State policymakers should work on efforts to make this happen.

IV.   Support prescribed burns to help manage forests

When the summer heat intensifies each year, peak fire season hits the western states hard. Consider the fact that Oregon (4), Idaho (5), Montana (9), and Washington (10) suffered more acres burned than most of the United States in 2022, all ranking in the top ten states of acreage burned in 2020 to 2022 (rank refers to 2022). Utah (21) and Wyoming (22) trailed slightly behind. Despite the ongoing fire danger and consequences, prescribed burns are used sparingly on federal lands in the mountain states.

Prescribed burning is underutilized in our region because the federal government owns the majority of public lands. Tribal and state agencies in the mountain states are increasing the funding for prescribed burns, but the area managed by these authorities is much smaller compared to federal lands. For example, 61.6% of Idaho lands are owned by the federal government and only 8.8% are owned by the state.

The federal government's feet dragging on prescribed burning keeps the mountain states from many positive benefits.[4] Historically, Native American tribes worked with nature to encourage fires where they were needed, managing fuel loads and deterring extreme fire behavior. However, a century of fire suppression tactics has increased the fuel load and combined with hotter and drier weather to create the extreme fire seasons the mountain states experience annually.

Despite this, tribes have been able to work within their smaller government systems to adopt prescribed burning practices and the results have returned once high-risk forests to healthier, historically correct states. But for federal-owned lands the battle is more cumbersome. Overwhelmed by red tape, lacking in generational knowledge of prescribed burns, and inundated with complaints of smoke inhalation and fire risk, federal lands still pursue mostly a fire suppression strategy. Fire resource budgets are almost entirely dedicated to suppressing fires no matter location or cause, and prescribed fires are rarely budgeted.

Federal lands in our region have a long way to go before they catch up on the long list of unhealthy forests. Millions of acres need treated but only thousands of acres are treated annually. It will take years of prescribed burns and harvesting to restore the western lands.

---

[4] "We're Not Doing Enough Prescribed Fire in the Western United States to Mitigate Wildfire Risk," MDPI, May 29, 2019, available at https://www.mdpi.com/2571-6255/2/2/30/htm

Important policies to improve forest health

Federal officials need to act now to adopt prescribed fire practices on a scale that can provide an actual solution to the growing pressure of unhealthy forests and excessive fuel loads. Policies that would improve the use of prescribed fires include:[5]

☐ Encouraging federal land agencies to request federal funding for sufficient fuel reduction projects and dedicating state-level funding;

☐ Ensure the EPA's Clean Air Act rule will not hinder the use of prescribed burns;

☐ Easing the permitting process so burn permits can be issued quickly (Idaho and Wyoming require longer than a day for authorization);

☐ Offer prescribed burn manager certification (only Washington offers it at this time); and

☐ Adopt a right-to-burn act, allowing private landowners to burn on their own land (only permitted in Oregon and Utah).

Unlike wildfire, new policies are difficult to move uphill, but prescribed burning is worth the push. Regional legislators have submitted multiple policies to remediate the western landscape, but progress has been sparse. The iconic forests of the mountain states need healthy, well-managed fire to thrive. Prescribed burning needs rapid and significant adoption to be beneficial to the mountain states' scenic region.

V.   Avoid trendy policies that have little environmental benefit

---

[5] "2021 National Prescribed Fire Use Survey Report," National Association of State Foresters, available at https://www.prescribedfire.net/pdf/2021-National-Rx-Fire-Use-Report_FINAL.pdf

A trend. A fad. Feel-good legislation. Call plastic bag bans whatever you want, just don't call them effective environmental policy.

Dozens of cities and states across the nation have either adopted or are considering adopting bans on plastics.

The question is whether banning plastic bags makes sense and can help the environment? The answer is likely no. In fact, much of the research shows plastic bags can be one of the most environmentally friendly options. There are numerous reasons for this.

First, plastic bags are reusable. Think about how many times you've reused a plastic bag to take a lunch to work, to clean up after your dog, or to fill a trash container in your bathroom. Without those bags available, consumers look for alternatives and end up buying *more* plastic bags.

The school of Forestry and Natural Resources at the University of Georgia released a study concluding:

> "The study found California communities with bag policies saw sales of 4-gallon trash bags increase by 55% to 75%, and sales of 8-gallon trash bags increase 87% to 110%."

Trash bag sales increased after grocery bag bans
University of Georgia

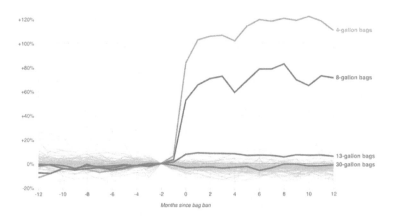

Second, the plastic bag alternatives are not much better. The United Kingdom's Environment Agency released a report in 2011 that highlighted the carbon impact of paper, reusable plastic, and cotton bags is *higher* than single-use plastic bags. In fact, scientists said you'd need to reuse a cotton bag more than 130 times to have an impact on the environment. Danish researchers had similar findings.

Third, there are sanitation concerns. Most people who carry around reusable, cloth bags do not necessarily take care to make sure the bag is clean. Some may keep the bag in their backseat or the trunk of their vehicle. Others might only wash the bag once a month. The concern about sanitation was especially high during the COVID-19 pandemic, when a number of states that had adopted bans decided to hold off because of hygiene concerns.

So, while plastic bag bans may make policymakers feel good, the research shows they are a very ineffective way to protect the environment and can actually do more harm than good. They should be avoided.

I. **Three keys for responsible transportation spending**

Transportation systems are the backbone of a strong local economy, allowing people and goods to move efficiently and effectively. At its core, transportation infrastructure is no different than any other type of public or private good and is subject to the law of supply and demand.

In the case of traffic congestion, the demand for road travel exceeds the supply of roads or capacity, the result of which leads to lost time, lost fuel, and excess pollutants emitted into the atmosphere.

Traffic congestion may also lead to capping growth and access while limiting labor markets. In essence, the number of available jobs, available workforce, and accessible services is limited by both distance and time. The more traffic congestion, the fewer opportunities to participate in the economy.

Freedom of mobility allows the public to travel wherever and how they choose with no – or minimal – restrictions. In recent decades, many public officials have waged campaigns to "discourage" certain modes, like cars, by implementing regressive tolling schemes, limiting parking, taking travel lanes away from drivers, and increasing traffic congestion to push people to other modes of transport or eliminate trips entirely.

Responsible transportation spending will be guided by policymakers who are guided by three key commitments.

1. Spend resources based on demand

Transportation spending should be guided by current and future demand instead of ideological visions. Politicians and transportation officials often want to spend limited tax and fee dollars based on how the public should travel instead of how the public chooses to travel.

For example, in Idaho, Valley Transit in the Treasure Valley seeks additional tax revenue to subsidize service, despite the lack of demand for its services.

According to the Metropolitan Planning Organization (MPO) for the Boise area, COMPASS, public transportation in the Valley will become insolvent around 2028, and by 2050, will have $328 million in deferred maintenance needs and $982 million in unfunded costs.

Yet in 2019, even before the COVID-19 pandemic, just 1,199 people took public transit as a commute mode, representing 0.4% of commuters, significantly lower than the 5.0% national average. To put this in perspective, 6.8% of people worked from home, and 88.8% of people commuted via car.

U.S. vs. Boise MSA commute mode share
2019

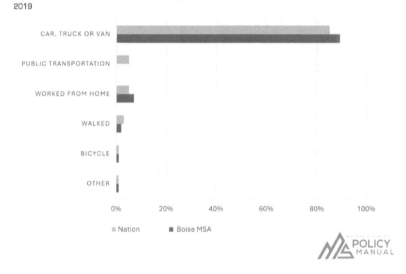

2. Users pay, users benefit

The highway system is largely funded by user fees, though in recent years transportation and politicians have dedicated sales tax revenues to the highway fund. User fees are collected by the federal, state, and local governments to maintain, preserve, and expand the road and highway system. Using Idaho as an example, taxes and fees include the $0.32 cents per gallon state fuel tax, the $0.184 cents per gallon federal fuel tax, and license fees.

The public transportation system in the Treasure Valley, Spokane region, and cities in Montana and Wyoming is, in part, funded by user fees, but the vast majority is paid by general taxation or deficit spending.

Due to the projected shortfall at public transportation agencies around Idaho, COMPASS officials have begun to analyze new "revenue streams," none of which involve users of the public transportation system paying more. Instead, they look to other options including a higher sales tax, or a vehicle-miles traveled fee, paid by drivers, which could be used to funnel money to other, less popular modes.

This same story is playing out across the Mountain States. Some argue that public transportation indirectly provides benefits to drivers by keeping cars off the road, leaving more space for everyone else. Yet road maintenance, preservation, and expansion provide a real, direct benefit to drivers instead of a theoretical, indirect benefit like transit.

3. Establish performance measures

As our region continues to grow, more pressure will continue to be put on the transportation network. It is important to establish performance measures whether for Interstates, state highways, local roads, or local public transportation, both in spending and ridership.

Looking to neighboring Washington state, official transportation policy goals once included things such as "delay on state highways should be significantly reduced and be no worse than the national mean," and, "delay per driver should be significantly reduced and be no worse than the national mean." Yet after stripping that policy goal from law, traffic congestion has continued to grow.

Other examples of policies that improve road and highway performance include maintaining a strong level of service standards and requiring that road projects maximize real-person throughput. Performance measures tied to revenue and spending can also benefit users. For example, if a passenger or commuter rail system is considered, it should be less costly and carry more riders than buses or a bus rapid transit line.

Recommended performance measures

Road	Reduce traffic delays and maintain competitiveness versus peer metro areas
Road	Maintain strong level of service standards for highways, arterials and city streets and intersections
Road	Maintain and increase actual person-throughput levels on roads and highways, not theoretical; increases traveler and economic benefits
Transit	Maintain minimum ridership per route, prioritize cuts where underused and commit to reinvestment
Transit	Match mode spending to performance
Transit	Keep costs per platform hour under national average and peer agencies
Transit	Implement minimum farebox recovery standards of 25%
Project selection	Ensure fair and adequate alternatives are studied with prioritization to most benefit/cost (and cost per rider, cost per user)
Project selection	Ensure projects selected are among the highest benefit-cost among potential projects using fair and accurate assumptions

By following these principles, policymakers will not only benefit travelers but also freight movers, suppliers and the even the agricultural industry.

II.   The most efficient and effective mass transit options

The primary goal of a mass transit system should be to move people from point A to point B in the most efficient manner possible. Both riders and taxpayers shoulder the burden of paying for public transit, but taxpayers typically cover most of the cost. Over the past decade, the price tag has only surged while ridership on most regional transit agencies has sharply declined.

Bus ridership
Spokane Transit Authority - 2012-2022

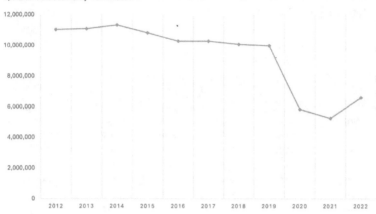

Bus ridership
Valley Regional Transit (Boise), City of Pocatello, Billings MET Transit, Butte Silver Bow Transit, 2012-2022
The National Transit Database – Federal Transit Administration

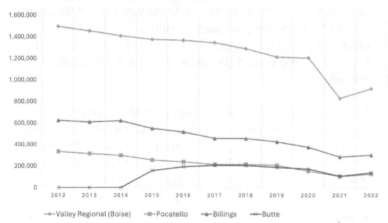

The largest transit agency in the region is Spokane Transit Authority (STA). Bus ridership has fallen precipitously since the early 2010's, with the most drastic fall coming in the wake of the COVID pandemic. The cost for STA's bus system, however, has only increased, with the cost per trip in 2022 hitting $11.41.

Cost Per Bus Ride

The National Transit Database – Federal Transit Administration

Year	Spokane Transit	Valley Regional (Boise)	City of Pocatello	Billings MET Transit	Butte Silver Bow Transit
2012	$3.92	$4.58	$3.26	$5.72	n/a
2013	$3.98	$4.97	$3.67	$6.01	n/a
2014	$4.02	$5.81	$4.05	$6.19	n/a
2015	$4.29	$6.01	$4.37	$7.25	$4.38
2016	$4.47	$6.99	$4.47	$6.92	$4.40
2017	$4.81	$7.85	$5.62	$7.67	$4.24
2018	$5.24	$8.27	$4.45	$8.22	$4.15
2019	$5.53	$8.99	$4.31	$9.16	$4.39
2020	$9.85	$9.41	$7.02	$10.68	$4.72
2021	$10.46	$13.82	$10.35	$15.15	$7.88
2022	$11.41	$14.36	$8.79	$14.65	$6.50
% Change	↑ 191%	↑ 214%	↑ 170%	↑ 156%	↑ 48%

Ridership declines are also seen at the primary transit agencies in Idaho and Montana. Unfortunately for taxpayers, the cost for providing a fewer number of rides is only increasing – up a staggering 214% in the past decade for Valley Regional Transit (Boise) and 191% for Spokane Transit.

The data for bus service only tells part of the story. Transit agencies also provide demand response service, which is a non-fixed route that is typically curb-to-curb and requires advanced scheduling. Often, passengers may have a disability that requires extra assistance. The cost to provide this service is enormous and only growing. In Spokane, Boise, Billings and Butte, demand response costs per trip can range from $40 to $60 – much more than a typical Uber or taxi might cost.

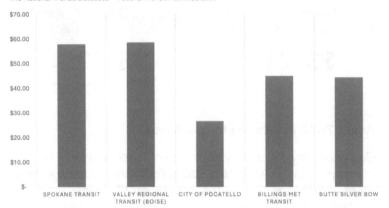

Demand Response Cost Per Trip
The National Transit Database – Federal Transit Administration

$70.00				
$60.00				
$50.00				
$40.00				
$30.00				
$20.00				
$10.00				
$-	SPOKANE TRANSIT	VALLEY REGIONAL TRANSIT (BOISE)	CITY OF POCATELLO	BILLINGS MET TRANSIT	BUTTE SILVER BOW

There is a success story in local public transit – vanpools. Much like a carpool, a vanpool is typically a group of 5-10 (sometimes more) people who commute to and from work together.

Vanpooling is cost effective as members will often share vehicle, gas, and any tolling costs. They pick the routes, the schedule, and the locations. And they also pick up a larger chunk of the tab.

Both Spokane Transit and the Ada County Highway District run successful vanpool programs that, in the end, cost a fraction of other modes, not only when looking at cost per trip but also the cost of transporting a passenger just one mile.

For Spokane Transit, the data shows a cost of $2.67 per mile on a bus. The cost to transport someone one mile via vanpoool is just $.28 – less than half the standard IRS mileage rate.

Vanpool Cost Per Trip
2022 – The National Transit Database – Federal Transit Administration

Spokane Transit	Ada Co. Highway District
$8.21	**$8.32**

III.   **Adopt Truth in Labeling for gas taxes**

Gas prices are inflated by government taxes and fees. Do consumers in the Mountain States really know what they are paying when they fill up at the gas station? The answer is likely no. That's because gasoline is one of the few products we purchase where taxes and fees are built into the price. This means there is no transparency about the true financial burden placed on consumers. The fix to this lack of transparency is what has been called "truth-in-labeling."

The Cost of Gasoline and taxes

Gas prices are difficult to predict. Most of the cost of a gallon of gas comes from the price of crude oil, which can fluctuate wildly. There are several components to the cost of a gallon of gas. The U.S. Department of Transportation says gas taxes make up about 19% of the overall cost of a gallon – but this will vary depending on the state and the current price.[1] For example, if the gas price is high, the gas tax percentage will be low. Likewise, if the gas price is low, the gas tax percentage could be much higher.

Gas taxes vary by state, but the Mountain States do charge more than average. In Idaho, the state gas tax is 32 cents per gallon. It was last increased in 2015. In Montana, the state gas tax costs consumers 31 cents per gallon. And in Washington, the state tax hits nearly 50-cents per gallon. Washington has also implemented a carbon tax and low carbon fuel standard that has dramatically increased the cost

---

[1] "Motor Fuel Data," U.S. Department of Transportation, available at
https://www.fhwa.dot.gov/policyinformation/motorfueldata.cfm

of a gallon of gasoline, although that policy is subject to repeal by voters in the 2024 general election.

The state-by-state tax burden does not include the federal gas tax of 18.4 cents per gallon. Overall, Idaho, Montana and Washington all have gas taxes that rank in the top 16 states. When taken together, a large portion of the overall cost of a gallon of gas goes toward taxes, which are mostly used to fund roads, bridges and a state's transportation system. However, when policymakers adopt gas tax hikes, there is no accountability built into the system. The cost is hidden in the price.

Federal and state gasoline taxes
January 2022

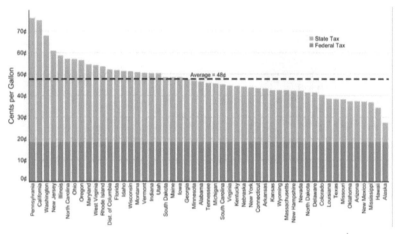

This is unusual when purchasing almost any product. After all, the price of a loaf of bread at the grocery store does not have the sales tax built in. Neither does the purchase of a bottle of water. Most consumers are able to see the tax burden they face on their receipts. If they don't like the cost or don't think it's being used properly, they can talk to their elected official. But with gas taxes, consumers are left in the dark.

Truth in Labeling examples from Washington, Ohio & Utah

In 2017, Washington state passed House Bill 2180, providing fuel tax transparency.[2] This measure required the Washington state Department of Agriculture to produce a sticker that would be placed on every gas pump near the weights and measures certification. The sticker would simply inform drivers of their state and federal tax burden. In Ohio, state workers began placing the stickers on gas pumps in 2019, as part of a deal to increase the gas tax.[3] In Utah, gas tax stickers are being placed at stations beginning this year.[4]

Gas tax transparency
The Idaho Poll – Mountain States Policy Center – November 2022

Would you support or oppose requiring the state to post, at the gas pump, how much it collects on each gallon of gasoline that is pumped?

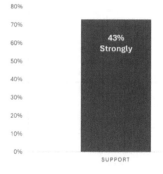

In most states, gas taxes are used to fund road construction projects. While not necessarily eager to pay more, taxpayers will typically support government funding that they know is

---

[2] "Knowing your gas tax cost," Seattle Times, November 2017, available at https://www.seattletimes.com/seattlenews/transportation/whats-your-gas-tax-stickers-coming-soon-to-the-pump/

[3] "Gas tax stickers finally being added to pumps," The Columbus Dispatch, February 11, 2020, available at https://www.dispatch.com/story/news/politics/2020/02/11/gas-tax-stickers-finally-being/1727809007/

[4] "Motor and special fuel tax act," Utah State Legislature, available at https://le.utah.gov/xcode/Title59/Chapter13/59-13-S201.html

transparent and will be wisely used. Unfortunately, gasoline taxes are not transparent. Because they are built into the cost of the product, citizens have no idea how much they are really paying, and where it is going. Inevitably, it makes it difficult for citizens to grasp the amount of funds available for transportation, and where they are being spent. In an age of surging gas prices, a "truth-in-labeling" policy is a reform worth pursuing.

IV. Avoid adopting a mileage tax

States and the federal government typically use gas taxes to pay for roads, bridges, highways and other transportation needs. But what happens when more Americans switch over to electric vehicles - who will pay then?

Transportation activists are telling the federal and state governments to adopt vehicle miles traveled (VMT) or, put simply, mileage taxes.[5]

In other words, you would be charged a certain amount for every mile that you drive. Some state proposals have the mileage tax at nearly three cents per mile. For the average person driving a vehicle 12,000 miles per year, that totals nearly $360.

In addition to the cost, there are many unanswered questions regarding a mileage tax, including:

☐ Would drivers be charged both gas taxes and mileage taxes?

☐ Would mileage taxes be required to be used on transportation projects?

☐ How would the government track a driver's mileage?

---

[5] "Keep it simple, experts tell feds on planned mileage fee experiment," Route Fifty, August 15, 2023, available at https://www.route-fifty.com/infrastructure/2023/08/keep-it-simple-experts-tell-feds-planned-mileage-fee-experiment/389449/

- ☐ How does the government avoid privacy concerns?

- ☐ Do mileage taxes unfairly punish those in rural communities?

In some state pilot programs, drivers have had the option of placing GPS devices in their vehicles to track mileage, but at least one participant also had her driving infractions recorded.[6]

But without a GPS or other form of tracking device to determine where you are driving, mileage reporting becomes a paperwork issue. If you live in a border community or take a long summer road trip, you could end up paying a tax to one state while driving on another state's roads.

Generally speaking, user fees are a solid and fair approach to transportation funding. However, use of a state or national mileage tax must first clearly answer these questions before being ready for implementation.

V.   Resist stifling rideshare regulations

The advancement of Uber, Lyft and other ridesharing services has revolutionized the way we move and provided an economic opportunity for thousands.

Unfortunately, policymakers in some regions have deemed it necessary for the government to get involved. In 2020, for example, the city of Seattle passed a "Fare Share" ordinance, which set minimum compensation for rideshare drivers.[7] Less than 24 months later, government leaders in Seattle decided

---

[6] "State may use private vehicle data for mileage tax," Washington Policy Center, December 15, 2021, available at
https://www.washingtonpolicy.org/publications/detail/state-may-use-private-vehicle-data-for-mileage-tax
[7] Minimum compensation established by Fare Share ordinance, Office of Seattle Mayor Jenny Durkan, January 2021, available at
https://durkan.seattle.gov/2021/01/minimum-compensation-established-by-fare-share-wage-ordinance-in-effect-as-of-january-2021/

to add more regulations – creating workplace "protections for app-based workers."[8]

The results have been disastrous. Prices for riders increased dramatically, which was particularly difficult for low income users. In fact, 44% of Uber rides start or end in a low-income neighborhood.

Those who drafted the legislation unintentionally set minimum compensation far higher than the minimum wage. As a result, demand fell and Seattle's trip cost recovery from the COVID shutdowns has been much lower than the rest of the United States.

Seattle rideshare trip cost recovery

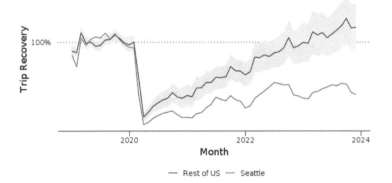

While the intentions behind the legislation are commendable, it's evident that policymakers in Seattle and elsewhere lack the necessary expertise to determine appropriate compensation for delivery drivers.

---

[8] The impact of Seattle's driver and courier pay regulations, Medium, February 22, 2024, available at https://medium.com/uber-under-the-hood/the-impact-of-seattles-driver-and-courier-pay-regulations-30fdc817e65c#:~:text=By%20failing%20to%20properly%20account,for%20a%20driver%20driving%2030mph.

These drivers provide a valuable service. They deserve fair pay. But companies like Uber, Lyft and DoorDash have established more effective methods for enabling people to enter the delivery business and for compensating them adequately.

Chris Cargill
President & CEO

For more than 20 years, Chris Cargill has worked in communications and public policy. Chris has deep roots in our region and is a graduate of Gonzaga University with a degree in broadcast communications and political science. His experience includes a decade in television news as well as 13 years for another state based think tank.

Chris' work has been published in the Idaho Statesman, The Coeur d'Alene Press, The Helena Independent Record, the Spokesman-Review, The Seattle Times, the Tri-City Herald and Real Clear Policy, as well as many other regional newspapers. He is also a familiar voice on radio stations throughout the region.

Chris is a member of the Heritage Foundation's Project 2025 Advisory Board, which is focused preparing comprehensive policy recommendations to ensure the next conservative presidential administration is prepared for success on day one. He is also a member of the American Enterprise Institute's Leadership Network.

Chris & his wife Lisa are the proud parents of two boys, including one who has special needs - one of the many reasons why he is so passionate about education choice options for families.

In his spare time, Chris spends time with family, serves on his local city council, and enjoys whatever down time he can in the great outdoors on his family property in North Idaho.

Jason Mercier
Vice President & Director of Research

Jason Mercier has more than 20 years'
experience working with public officials,
media, and citizen stakeholders across
the nation to improve the fiscal,
governance and transparency policies of
local and state governments. He spent
the last 16 years as the Director of the
Center for Government Reform at
Washington Policy Center.

Jason has been appointed by lawmakers
and governors to various tax, budget
and transparency reform committees.
He is a Fellow with the national Better Cities Project and is also a
member of the State Tax Advisory Board for the Tax Foundation.
Jason has testified numerous times before legislative committees
across the country on government reform issues, and his op-eds
have been published in numerous newspapers across the region.

When he's not geeking out on studies and audits, Jason's life revolves
around his wife and two daughters and the 49ers' schedule.

Madilynne Clark
Senior Policy Analyst

Madilynne Clark holds a master's degree in Agricultural and
Resource Economics from Colorado State University as well as a B.S.
in Environmental Economics, Policy, and Management from Oregon
State University.

Madi's work has been published in The Capital Press, Tri-City Herald,
and the Spokesman-Review and she has spoken to agricultural
groups across the Pacific Northwest.

A small farmer, and a mom to four boys, Madi is the daughter of a large-animal veterinarian. She grew up on many different farms. Each farm faced its own challenges, which required unique solutions. She learned early on that a one-size-fits-all approach will never work - not for farmers and not for families.

Madi and her husband, Kyler, returned to their home state of Oregon four years ago. They live, farm, and raise their boys only a few miles from the Idaho border.

Amber Gunn
Senior Policy Analyst

Amber Gunn is the former Director of Economic Policy for the Olympia-based Freedom Foundation. She has served as a voting member on the American Legislative Exchange Council's (ALEC) Tax and Fiscal Policy Task Force and has been a resource to media outlets and legislative staff for issue briefs and policy analysis.

During her time with ALEC, Amber co-authored the organization's influential State Budget Reform Toolkit, which provided budget and procurement best practices to guide state policymakers in all 50 states as they worked to solve budget shortfalls.

Her work has been featured in the Seattle Times, Investor's Business Daily, Seattle Business, The Street, The Olympian, The Tacoma News Tribune, the Spokesman-Review, and many other. news outlets. Her research and analysis has been cited and used by King 5 Investigators, KOMO 4 News, KIRO 7 News, Northwest Public Radio, and various talk radio shows and radio news outlets.

Amber was a Charles G. Koch Fellow in partnership with the State Policy Network and the Institute for Humane Studies.

Sebastian Griffin
Director, Junkermier Center for Technology & Innovation

Sebastian Griffin is a 5th generation Idahoan and Nampa native. He current serves as MSPC's Marketing and Communications coordinator, and is the lead researcher for MSPC's Junkermier Center on Technology and Innovation.

He is married to his high school sweetheart and has a daughter named Wyld. Sebastian graduated from Nampa High, the College of Western Idaho with his Associate's Degree in Liberal Arts, and Boise State with a Bachelor's Degree in Political Science and American Government.

He has been involved in the policy making process in Idaho for the last five years starting as a Senate Page and most recently as a Legislative Candidate in Idaho's District 12. He also serves on the Nampa City Council.

Bob Pishue
Visiting Fellow

Visiting Fellow Bob Pishue is based in Boise and is currently the Transportation Analyst and head of Research at the global traffic data and analytics company INRIX.

Bob's research and analysis have been featured in key media outlets such as The Wall Street Journal, Fox News, CNN, BBC, Forbes, and The Washington Post, among others.

He has extensive experience in state and local transportation policy, and was formerly the Director of Transportation for Kemper Development Company, a prominent property developer in Washington state and was previously the Transportation Director at Washington Policy Center, a non-partisan free-market think tank.

Dr. Roger Stark
Visiting Fellow

Dr. Roger Stark is a retired physician and author of three books including *Healthcare Policy Simplified: Understanding a Complex Issue*, and *The Patient-Centered Solution: Our Health Care Crisis, How It Happened, and How We Can Fix It*.

He has also authored numerous in-depth studies on health care policy including *Efforts at Reform in Other States, What Works and What Doesn't: A Review of Health Care Reform in the States*, and *Health Care Reform that Works: An Update on Health Savings Accounts*.

Over a 12-month period in 2013 and 2014, Dr. Stark testified before three different Congressional committees regarding the Affordable Care Act. Dr. Stark graduated from the University of Nebraska's College of Medicine and he completed his general surgery residency in Seattle and his cardiothoracic residency at the University of Utah.

After practicing in Tacoma he moved to Bellevue and was one of the co-founders of the open-heart surgery program at Overlake Hospital.

He has been a member of many regional and national professional organizations and currently makes his home in Utah.

Olivia Johnston
Contributor

Olivia Johnston is the author of a quarterly column in MSPC's Pinnacle magazine called "On the Law."

Olivia is a graduate of the University of Idaho College of Law. She earned her undergraduate degree in Business Administration from Gonzaga University.

In 2021, she was the recipient of the Jennifer Dunn Thompson scholarship, named after former Congresswoman Jennifer Dunn. The honor is awarded annually to women with a promise in policy work.

Sam Cardwell
Contributor

Sam Cardwell is an alumnus of the University of Washington and Liberty University, obtaining a bachelor's degree in political science. Sam has worked on multiple legislative and congressional campaigns across Washington State.

Sam is the author of several MSPC studies, including *Adopting a new income tax liability threshold* and *Powering the Mountain States: A snapshot of the region's energy portfolio*.

JOIN MSPC!

Mountain States Policy Center is a 501c3 non-profit charity. We are funded by citizens, families, business owners and more from across the region. Contributions to MSPC are tax-deductible to the fullest extent permitted by law. Our federal tax identification number is 88-2607055.

There are many ways to support the organization. You may choose to give a one-time gift, join the Freedom Circle with a monthly gift, donate stock, or even join our major giving program The Summit Club.

$50-250
Member
Invites to all events
Weekly email updates
Subscription to Pinnacle magazine

$250-1,000
Free Marketeer
Invites and discounts to all events
Weekly email updates
Subscription to Pinnacle magazine
Exclusive opportunities with key policymakers

$1,000-$2,500
Sustainer
Invites and discounts to all events
Weekly email updates
Subscription to Pinnacle magazine
Exclusive opportunities with key policymakers
Recognition at all MSPC events

$2,500-5,000
Free Market Champion
Invites and discounts to all events
Weekly email updates
Subscription to Pinnacle magazine
Exclusive opportunities with key policymakers
Recognition at all MSPC events
Private lunch opportunities with keynote speakers

Scan this code to join MSPC with a tax-deductible gift!

Made in United States
Troutdale, OR
10/18/2024

23866819R00100